BONFIRE BODIES

The shocking story of serial killer Dennis Nilsen

Robert Brown

Copyright © Robert Brown- 2019

Paperback Edition

All rights reserved.

No part of this publication may be reproduced, stored in a retrieval system, or transmitted, without the prior written permission by the author.

This is based on a true story. No names have been changed, however, some of the dialogue, thoughts and conversations between people have been altered to give the reader a clearer picture of the events that took place.

Disclaimer: The material in this publication has a strong adult theme and is intended for an adult audience.

Reader discretion is advised.

CONTENTS

PROLOGUE 1
CHAPTER 1 3
CHAPTER 2 8
CHAPTER 3 13
CHAPTER 4 18
CHAPTER 5 25
CHAPTER 6 30
CHAPTER 7 33
CHAPTER 8 39
CHAPTER 9 44
CHAPTER 10 47
CHAPTER 11 55
CHAPTER 12 62
CHAPTER 13 68
CHAPTER 14 71
CHAPTER 15 78
CHAPTER 16 85
CHAPTER 17 88
CHAPTER 18 93
CHAPTER 19 98
CHAPTER 20 103
CHAPTER 21 107
CHAPTER 22 115
CHAPTER 23 123
CHAPTER 24 137

CHAPTER 25	147
EPILOGUE	150
ABOUT THE AUTHOR	155
MORE BOOKS BY ROBERT BROWN	156

PROLOGUE

"We, the jury, find the defendant, Dennis Andrew Nilsen, guilty of six counts of murder in the first degree and guilty of two counts of attempted murder."

Dennis Nilsen stared at the jury foreman with cold eyes, thinking: *Six killings that the prosecution can prove, sure. What about the other six?*

He knew for a fact that he had murdered at least twelve young men, more likely fifteen. He wasn't sure about the exact number because he couldn't remember every one of his victims in detail. Some vividly, yes, but not all of them. On a number of blurry days, Dennis had been too drunk to even ask for, or recall, the names of his victims.

The jury foreman was still citing the details of his crimes, but Dennis Nilsen wasn't paying attention anymore. He gazed out the window and watched the reflection of the grey winter clouds in the surface of the River Thames. Standing in the dock of the Old Baily Central Criminal Court in London, he couldn't understand how it had taken the jury nearly two days to deliberate over his fate.

He had confessed everything to the police and there was nothing substantial to deny his guilt. Transcripts of his confessions and various interviews by the authorities – lasting more than thirty hours in total – have been read out in court by the prosecution's lawyers. In one of these conversations with a police investigator, Dennis had even said, "I have no tears for my victims. I have no tears for myself, nor those bereaved by my actions."

It was him, all right.

He was the killer.

It was all over London's newspapers, even though publishing this was in contempt of the court, and everybody in England knew he was guilty.

His defense attorney had come up with some bullshit story about "mental disorder", to get him off on manslaughter only, but that was quickly nipped in the bud by the judge. In his summation, the judge had instructed the jury to dispense with the psychiatric jargon and take into consideration that a mind could be evil without being abnormal. "There are evil people who do evil things," the judge had said. "Committing murder is one of them. There must be no excuses for moral defects."

Dennis sighed as he returned his gaze to the imposing figure of the jury foreman, who had finished reading the verdict and was now awaiting further instructions from the judge. The cold and stuffy courtroom was silent as a grave.

Less than two miles away, the Great Bell of Big Ben's clock rang out five times and a shiver ran down Dennis Nilsen's spine. The afternoon was coming to a close and Londoners were beginning to make their way home after yet another day of hard work. Dennis knew he would never be one of these free folk again. He knew he was going to spend the rest of his life in prison.

I deserve that much, he thought. *I brought it on myself.*

He could have done so many things differently.

He could have had such a different life.

***

Later, as he was taken to Her Majesty's Prison Wormwood Scrubs in a marked police vehicle, Dennis Nilsen shook his head and a feeling of utter disgust washed over him.

How did I end up here? he silently asked himself.

How did it all come to this?

The answer was simple.

One had to go back thirty-three years in time to find out.

CHAPTER 1

Dennis Nilsen's troubles began when he was only five years old, in the fall of 1951.

On a mild day late in October, his grandfather, Andrew Whyte – who had just returned from a four week fishing trip in the North Sea – was talking to his mother, Betty Nilsen, in the kitchen. The kitchen door was open and Dennis, who was sitting on one of the faded burgundy couches in the living room, could hear everything that was being said by the two adults.

"Where is Olav?" his grandfather asked his mother.

"He is visiting a friend," Betty replied. "I don't expect him back before dusk."

Dennis grinned. Olav, his older brother, was playing marbles at Mikey's house, a few blocks down the road from their home. The fact that Mother wasn't expecting Olav back soon meant that Dennis would go on the countryside walk with Grandpa by himself. Mother would never allow Sylvia to go along if Olav wasn't with them. She wasn't old enough, yet. Sylvia was their sister and the youngest of the three Nilsen siblings.

This thought excited Dennis. His grandfather was his hero and his grand protector. He liked it very much to spend time alone with old Andrew.

"Don't you want to come with us, Betty?" he heard his grandfather ask. "It's such a fine afternoon."

Dennis stared through the window. It was indeed a fine autumn afternoon in Scotland, a country that was usually cold, wet and miserable. Today, the sun was shining through a few puffy clouds and he could smell the salty sea breeze blowing in from the harbour.

"No, please, Dad," his mother's voice sounded from the kitchen. "You know me and me buggered hip. I won't make it past two miles." She gave a nervous laugh.

"All right," said Andrew, "looks like it's just Dennis and I then."

Young Dennis Nilsen's grin widened into a broad smile, exposing a gap where his two front baby teeth had shed. He couldn't wait for his permanent teeth to erupt; it was difficult to chew liquorice with only his back teeth. The goo kept on sticking to the uneven surface of the molars and then he had to use his dirty fingers to dig it out.

His grandfather walked into the lounge and announced: "Let's go, young man! The sun waits for no one, you know?" He held out his arms in front of him.

Dennis leapt up and ran into Andrew's arms. "I missed you so much Grandpa!" he cried out.

That was the truth.

Since Dennis had never known his father, Andrew Whyte was like a father to him. His mother had divorced his biological father after Sylvia had been born and Dennis was not even three years old at the time, too young to have any recollection of any events prior to the divorce. To him, Grandpa was his only father; he had never known another one. Whenever Andrew went on his extended fishing trips, Dennis felt empty and sad. Make no mistake, he loved Grandma Lily, but he loved Grandpa Andrew so much more.

His grandfather took his hand and led him outside, where the fresh air of the tiny town of Fraserburgh, Aberdeenshire, greeted them. Dennis was wearing only a short-sleeved chequered shirt and a green pair of corduroy shorts, but he did have his jersey tied around his waist. By the time they would return, it would be close to sunset and a little chilly. That's what Grandpa always said before they went on their countryside walks.

"Can I ride on your shoulders again, Grandpa?" Dennis asked, his chocolate brown eyes wide with anticipation.

"Of course, my big boy," replied Andrew. He pulled his grandson up with one arm and placed him on his shoulders, grabbing hold of the boy's thin ankles in front of his chest.

Ahead of them, recently mowed lawns painted the neighborhood in a lush green postcard picture and Dennis could hear a flock of seagulls squawking in the distance.

They made their way down to the docks, first on Frithside Street, then right onto Shore Street and finally left onto Harbour Road. Here, the wind was a bit stronger but not cold by any stretch of the imagination. Not if you were a Scottish lad like Dennis. He gazed at the herring fishing boats in the harbour and pointed at a specific one with his index finger. "Is *that* your fishing trailer, Grandpa?" he asked excitedly.

Andrew chuckled. "Not *trailer*, my boy, *trawler*. And, yes, that is the fishing trawler I usually work on. You have a good memory, Dennis."

"Thanks, Grandpa," Dennis replied. He rubbed his chin and muttered, "Trawler. Fishing trawler."

"Do you want to go all the way up to Inverallochy again?" asked Andrew.

Inverallochy was a picturesque little fishing village, four miles east of the Fraserburgh harbour, just past Cairnbulg.

"Yes, please!" exclaimed Dennis. Then his voice grew sombre. "How long are you staying this time, Grandpa?" he asked.

"Oh, just about two days or so," Andrew replied quietly. At sixty-two, he was tired and in poor health. The long years at sea had taken its toll on his body. He had told his wife, Lily, that his next fishing trip was going to be his last before he was going to retire. He was getting too old for the sea now.

They continued further along the harbour, past the golf course and onto the long stretch of white sand leading to Philorth Beach. Beyond this beach stood a number of high sand dunes, hiding Inverallochy from their view. Dennis climbed off his grandfather's shoulders to run up and down the dunes, while Andrew sat down on the beach to catch his breath.

When Dennis was eventually tired, he slumped down beside his grandfather and peered into the distance. "What is on that side of the world, Grandpa?" he asked, frowning.

Andrew followed his gaze south and said, "That, young Dennis, is England, the biggest country in the entire United Kingdom."

The boy's eyes lit up. "Oh, I know about England! The capital is Landon and–"

"London," his grandfather corrected him.

"London," Dennis Nilsen repeated.

Little did he know then how much misery and carnage he was going to cause in London three decades later...

After taking a stroll through Inverallochy, they returned to Betty Nilsen's house just before sunset and Andrew stayed for supper.

When they had finished their meals, he turned to his grandson. "So, are you looking forward to going to primary school next year?"

Dennis shook his head. "I'm scared, Grandpa."

"Don't be scared," his mother told him. "You're a clever boy, Dennis. You will get used to it in no time, I promise." She pointed her chin at his plate, where two fish fingers remained. "Are you going to finish that?"

Grabbing the two fish fingers with his right hand, Dennis replied, "They're for my birds." He pulled on his grandfather's sleeve with his left hand. "Come, Grandpa. I want to show you."

Andrew stood up and followed his grandson to his room.

Dennis sat down at his study desk and cautiously opened the drawer. Inside, in a makeshift dishcloth nest, were two baby finches.

Biting off a chunk of fish finger, Dennis masticated it with his remaining teeth before feeding it to the birds from his mouth, like he was their mother.

After praising him for taking such good care of the animals, Andrew hugged him, ruffled his short brown hair playfully, then said goodbye and left.

That was the last time Dennis Nilsen saw his grandfather alive.

CHAPTER 2

On the day of Halloween, 1951, three weeks before his sixth birthday, Dennis Nilsen came home from kindergarten to find his mother crying on a couch in the lounge.

After the bus had dropped him off, he ran into the house and then stopped in his tracks. He dropped his lunchbox to the floor and hurried over to his mother. "What is it, Mommy," he asked in a hushed voice.

She looked up at him with red eyes and said, "Grandpa is here."

Dennis was confused. Why would his mother by crying if Grandpa had returned from the sea earlier than expected?

"Come," she told him, rising to her feet. "Let us go to Grandpa."

He followed her through the corridor and into the kitchen.

Andrew Whyte lay in a wooden coffin on the large kitchen table, his eyes closed and his hands folded across his chest like a saint. He was dressed in a black suit with a white shirt and a black bowtie.

Dennis ran toward the table crying, "Grandpa! Grandpa!"

"Shhh," his mother cautioned him. "Grandpa is sleeping, Dennis."

Upon reaching the old man, Dennis instantly knew something was seriously wrong with his hero. Although not yet old enough to understand the concept of death, he had a suspicion that his beloved grandfather was very, very ill. Andrew's face was pallid and swollen, his lips were purple, his mouth was half-open and his usual raspy breaths could not be heard anymore. Something terrible was wrong, Dennis knew, but there was nothing he could do to help Grandpa. He realized at that moment that the old man wasn't going to wake up from his deep sleep. When he interrogated his mother about this "sleep", she told him that Grandpa had gone to a better place.

Why didn't he take me with him to this better place? young Dennis Nilsen's mind argued.

Three days later, on the day of the funeral, he found out from Olav and his friends that his grandfather had died from a heart attack while at sea and that his body had been brought ashore and returned to the family home prior to the burial. Olav's friends explained to Dennis in gory detail the difference between life and death.

Standing beside the grave in the fog, weeping, little Dennis now knew exactly what death was, but his five-year-old brain simply could not process the idea that his grandfather, whom he'd loved so much, would never return to earth.

Much later in his life, Dennis Nilsen would state that this had been the most traumatic event of his life and that it had been there, at the burial, when his concept of love and death converged together into a hazy mess of misperception.

***

After his grandfather's death, Dennis became an introvert who never opened up to any adults and rarely to children his own age. His sister, Sylvia, was an exception. He sometimes shared his emotions with her, but only sometimes.

He would often go down to the harbour to watch the trawlers offload their catch and during summers he would go for a swim in the sea all by himself.

On one such an occasion, when he was nine years old, he nearly drowned.

With a spring tide looming, the current was especially strong that day, reeling him into the deep waters in the nick of time. Dennis began to shout, "Help! Somebody help me!" while waving his arms in the air. He looked around in panic and when he couldn't see anybody anywhere around him, he started yelling louder. "I'm drowning! I'm, drowning! HELP!" Then he submerged beneath the water, thinking it was all over. Just as he was about to gasp for air that wasn't there, an older boy grabbed him around the chest and pulled him up, effectively rescuing his life.

Dennis never remembered his rescuer's name, but he vividly recalled the strong boy's hands and smooth body touching him all over as they had made it back to shore. He thought about that a lot and, in his mind, he was also growing up pretty fast. He began to explore his body more and more, and by the time he was twelve years old, Dennis Nilsen was an avid masturbator.

On a summer day in 1957, after a family picnic with his mother and siblings in the Scottish countryside, Dennis returned home to find that everybody was exhausted except for him. He pulled on his pyjamas and climbed into bed, but he just wasn't able to fall asleep.

Later, on his way to the kitchen to fetch a glass of milk, Dennis noticed that the door to Olav's room was slightly ajar. He listened for any sounds and when he was satisfied that everybody in the house was fast asleep, he entered his brother's room. He quietly tip-toed across the carpeted floor and knelt down beside Olav's bed. Pulling the blankets aside, he slowly slid his hand into his brother's pyjama pants. The large penis he felt in there wasn't exceptionally hard or overly soft; it was semi-erect and the texture felt like a large unpeeled banana to Dennis. He spent a few moments playing with the genitals and then stood up, his heart beating viciously in his chest.

By the time Dennis had returned to his room, the crotch of his pyjama pants was soaking wet with semen.

That was the night he realized he was hooked on boys.

That was the night he found out that he was a homosexual.

***

Life took a few turns after 1957.

His mother married another man, a guy whom Dennis didn't like at all, and they moved to Strichen, a small town twenty miles south of their old home.

One evening, the three children were alone at home while their mother and stepfather had gone out for dinner. A friend of Olav pitched up at the house shortly after the adults had left. Olav was a popular boy in school and, contrary to Dennis, had plenty of friends. Dennis envied his brother's popularity and could never quite grasp how certain boys, like himself, didn't have any real close friends. The majority of *his* friends were imaginary ones; tall and lean with smooth bodies.

"We're leaving," Olav told him. "There is a bonfire party at the beach for *older* children. We'll be back before Mom and the slave driver gets home."

"You can't," replied Dennis. "Mom said we must both look after Sylvie."

"Why is he such a bitch?" Olav's friend asked, staring at Dennis.

Olav grinned. "Because *he* is the little hen in the house, not Sylvie over there."

Dennis Nilsen's stomach made a backflip.

Up to that moment, he had never realized Olav knew about his secret. He had been trying to keep the fact that he had gay tendencies from the rest of the world. As a twelve-year-old boy, he had enough on his plate in dealing with puberty and the shame of his homosexuality – which was still very much taboo in the late 1950s – and now there was the added pressure of his brother telling everybody at school about his sexual orientation.

Later that evening, when he was alone in the house with his sister, he fondled Sylvia in an effort to get rid of his affection for boys but it didn't work. After explaining to Sylvia that boys and girls needed to "explore" each other, she agreed to take off her clothes but the more Dennis touched her, the more his feelings for the opposite sex diminished.

Over the next four years, Betty Nilsen was constantly pregnant and had another four children with Dennis' stepfather. The house was becoming crowded and Dennis didn't like his life anymore. They were poor, there was almost no entertainment in the depressing town of Strichen, and the closest beach was twenty miles away. His stepfather was mean to him and, in his mind, his mother was giving too much attention to the younger children.

He wanted out.

CHAPTER 3

"What do mean you're going to join the army?" asked Betty Nilsen. She was sitting across from her son at a small coffee shop in town.

Dennis took a sip of his coffee and shrugged. "I can't stay in the house forever, Ma," he said. "I have to start living my own live at some point and now is as good a time as ever." He had brought his mother to the coffee shop to get away from the hullabaloo of all the toddlers in the house.

"But you're only fifteen years old!" Betty protested. However, she didn't have a lot of ground to stand on. This was the year 1961 and many young men under the age of eighteen were enlisted in the United Kingdom's army.

"Fifteen years *young*, Ma," Dennis replied, smiling.

Defeated, she looked down at her unpainted fingernails and asked, "Which Division are you planning on joining, son?"

Dennis Nilsen's smile brightened. "The Catering Corps," he said. "I'm going to become an army chef. That is my goal. I will get free board and lodging and they pay good wages."

He had practiced these sentences over and over in front of the bathroom mirror the previous evening, and now it was time to show his mother he could be independent and responsible for his own life. In reality, he just wanted to get away from the crowded house, away from his strict stepfather and the hell away from the boring town of Strichen.

The chef-trick worked, Dennis noticed. Now that his mother understood that he wasn't going to war to die on some battlefield it seemed to soothe her nerves.

Betty sat back in her chair and her face grew serious. "Are you sure this is what you want to do?"

"Absolutely," Dennis answered. "I'll be all right, Ma. Don't worry about me."

So, off to the army he went.

He commenced his training with the Army Catering Corps at St. Omer Barracks in Aldershot, forty miles southwest of London.

The next three years were the happiest years of Dennis Nilsen's life.

Although he couldn't stand the physical training, the camaraderie at the barracks was something he had never experienced before. Everybody was friendly with him and accepted him the way he was. No one pushed him away like his brother's friends had done when he had been in school. Some of his colleagues regarded him as odd, but they never made fun of him. While they were all listening to The Beatles and The Rolling Stones, Dennis was into classical music; Beethoven, Bach, Vivaldi and Mozart. And while his mates read the popular *Parade* magazines, he was reading poetry and writing stories; sometimes even constructing his own poems.

His homosexuality remained a secret, since it was illegal for gays to enlist in the military during the 1960s. Instead of using the communal open shower facilities, Dennis always bathed alone in one of the enclosed adjoining bathrooms. He was too afraid of getting an erection if he dared to shower with his fellow recruits and, besides, the privacy of the bathrooms gave him the opportunity to masturbate without any interference.

He bought an expensive camera with his first paycheck and became a self-proclaimed photographer in Aldershot. This allowed him to live out some of his fantasies without taking too much of a risk.

Late in the evenings, before lights-out, he would gather some colleagues around and say, "All right, boys, we're going to do a battle scene." The other trainee soldiers thought he was weird but they played along – it was an interesting alternative to the otherwise boring evenings in the barracks.

"You two," Dennis would say, his camera dangling from its leather strap around his neck, "on the floor with your arms above your heads. You've been slain in battle."

"What about me?" a third colleague would ask.

"Sit against the foot of this bed," Dennis would instruct. "Put your rifle's barrel in your mouth. You committed suicide because you couldn't handle the gruesomeness of the war anymore."

Then Dennis would take pictures of these men posing dead and later, once the photos had been developed, masturbate over them in the bathroom.

It was an exciting time and he enjoyed manipulating these young soldiers in his photoshoot sessions. He had long forgotten about stupid Strichen, where his mother and his stupid stepfather and his six siblings were struggling along.

In July 1964, he passed his catering exam and was officially assigned to the first Battalion of the Royal Fusiliers in Osnabrück, West Germany. Here, eighteen-year-old Dennis Nilsen – now a grown man standing over six feet tall and weighing in at two-hundred-and-ten pounds – started smoking cigarettes and discovered his love for alcohol.

He drank copious amounts of beer and gluhwein almost every night, until he passed out, and the intake of alcohol made him less shy about his sexual orientation. He would hang around the necks of his colleagues and allow them to hug him and carry him to bed when he was unable to stand anymore. On many occasions, he pretended to be passed out in the hope of someone making sexual use of his body but, sadly for Dennis, this never happened.

He was stationed in West Germany for two years, then returned to Aldershot for a brief couple of months before he was deployed to Norway and then to Aden, Yemen, to serve as a cook at one of the prisons. Here in Yemen, he didn't have to stay in a barracks, he had his own room in the compound.

Around the corner from the army compound was an antique shop where Dennis bought two important items to enhance his sexual fantasies: a freestanding mirror and an oil-painted copy of *The Raft of the Medusa* by Théodore Géricault. The painting depicted some survivors of a shipwreck on a small raft and it was the image in the bottom left hand corner that interested Dennis. Sitting on the edge of the raft was an old man with the naked body of a dead youngster in his lap. Beside them was another dead man with the lower half of his torso missing.

Dennis positioned the painting and the mirror beside his bed in such a way that, when he lay on the bed, only the lower half of his body reflected in the mirror. He would then masturbate while shifting his stare back and forth, between the naked dead man in the painting and his own nude squirming body, pretending to have anal intercourse with another male.

This became an afternoon ritual he carried out every day after lunch.

After performing the ritual for two months, his fantasies finally became a reality when he befriended a young Arab man with whom he engaged in homosexual acts on a number of occasions.

Dennis never learned how to speak Arabic, but he made friends in the Middle East quite easily because everybody enjoyed his western cooking recipes; especially the mean curry he sometimes prepared for the prisoners and guards. He loved spending time in the kitchen and cooking had become a form of art in his mind by then.

One night, after a heavy drinking session in one of Aden's bars, Dennis hailed a taxi back to the prison and, as soon as he climbed in, was hit over the head with a hard object and lost consciousness. When he awoke, he was in the trunk of the taxi as it came to a halt. The trunk was opened by a well-built Arab man and Dennis pretended to be asleep while the man dragged him out of the car. When his body was halfway out, Dennis Nilsen grabbed a jack-handle from the floor of the trunk and knocked the taxi driver to the ground before beating him to a pulp. He then locked the Arab man in the taxi's trunk and hitchhiked back to the prison. He never heard what happened to the taxi driver after that.

***

After Yemen, Nilsen went back to Britain and was deployed to Plymouth with the Argyll and Sutherland Highlanders at Seaton Barracks for a year. Then he was transferred to Cyprus and eventually back to Germany in 1969, a week after Neil Armstrong and Buzz Aldrin had landed the Apollo 11 Lunar Module on the moon.

In Berlin, Nilsen hired a prostitute and had his first sexual experience with a female. Though he bragged about the encounter with his fellow soldiers afterwards, he regarded this "regular" intercourse as extremely boring, depressing and overrated. It was not at all like his vivid fantasies about passive and vulnerable male counterparts.

His final three years in the army saw him travel to Inverness, Scotland and then to the Shetland Islands, where he was equipped to film the beautiful landscapes with a Kodak 8mm motion film camera. Once again, he used his fellow soldiers as actors "playing dead".

A violent fight with one of his roommates on the Shetland Islands eventually brought about the termination of Dennis Nilsen's military services in October 1972.

Upon returning to his family in Strichen, he told them he had left the army on his own accord, because he wasn't happy with the way the British soldiers had shot unarmed civilians during a protest march on Bloody Sunday, January 30th 1972 in Derry, Northern Ireland.

His brother, Olav, didn't believe this story.

CHAPTER 4

"When are you going to get a job, Dennis?" Betty Nilsen asked.

They were having a Sunday lunch in her home in Strichen; she, Olav and his wife, Dennis, and two of the younger siblings. It was late in November and mighty cold outside. Olav had made a fire in the dining room's fireplace and the atmosphere inside was cosy and tranquil.

"I'm thinking of going to London to join the police force, Ma," Dennis answered. He had been living in his mother's house for over a month after returning from the Shetland Islands.

"And why are you so hopeless at getting a girlfriend?" Betty asked, chewing lamb shank in-between her questions. "You are twenty-seven years old for God's sake."

"Because he's a bloody faggot," Olav blurted out.

Dennis felt his face flush. He couldn't believe his brother had just said that.

Betty raised an eyebrow. "A what?"

"A faggot, Ma," Olav repeated. "You know, a queer. He likes boys instead of girls."

"Oh my," said Betty, taking short breaths. "Is that true Dennis?"

Pushing his plate aside, Dennis stood up and muttered, "Thanks for the food," before standing up and going into the lounge to smoke a cigarette.

He was furious with Olav.

The previous evening they had watched a movie called *Victim*, about the discovery of a blackmail plot against several gay men in the 1960s, London. Olav and his wife had made it clear that they hated homosexuals. Dennis had experienced this as a personal insult and he and his brother had a brawl after the movie. Now, Olav had just gone too far by telling their mother about his sexual orientation. *And in such a vulgar way*. Dennis felt as if he could strangle Olav with his bare hands.

He moved to London a week later and began his training at the Metropolitan Police Academy.

A career in uniform seemed like a natural progression after he had been in the army for eleven years, more than a third of his life so far.

***

He completed his training sixteen months after that, in April 1973, and began working as a junior constable at a police station in Willesden Green, northwest London. He was given free accommodation at the Police Section House, so he spent all his earnings on clothing, food and booze.

At first, he sincerely missed the companionship of his army colleagues, but he soon got into the groove and evolved into an efficient uniformed police officer by day, and a casually dressed "seeker of attractive men" by night.

The rock band Queen had taken England by storm in 1973 and Freddy Mercury's image had changed the gay scene in London dramatically. There were hundreds of gay pubs everywhere and homosexuality was exposed more and more to the public. Dennis enjoyed the buzzing London nightlife and engaged in a number of sexual relations with gay men during his time as a junior constable. However, all of these encounters were one-night stands – or weekend occurrences at best – and did not satisfy Nilsen's need for a steady partner. He was lonely and in search of a more permanent relationship.

He was now growing out of his love for classical music and began to listen to Rock and Pop bands such as The Who, Led Zeppelin and the Edgar Winter Group. He also gradually progressed from drinking beer to hard liquor such as whiskey and rum. Dennis was particularly fond of dark rum with Coca Cola, a drink many policemen in England enjoyed at the time.

His biological father died in August that year and he was surprized to receive a check for £1,000 as his portion of the inheritance.

By December 1973, Dennis Nilsen couldn't stand the guilt of being a police officer and a man frequenting gay pubs at the same time anymore. He had seen dozens of men behaving indecently in public, usually in alleys behind these pubs, and he could never bring himself to arrest them.

He resigned from the police force and worked as a contracting security guard at various Crown properties for six months, all the time on the lookout for a more permanent position.

During these months, he was effectively "homeless" because he didn't have the luxury of staying at the Police Section House anymore. He slept in hostels, rented rooms on a week-by-week basis, and eventually ended up with a longer-term lease agreement in a room on Teignmouth Road, in the Cricklewood district of London.

The security guard jobs bored Dennis to death, but it generated income to pay for food and lodging. He was keeping his inheritance money in the bank for the time when he could obtain a stable job and move into an apartment.

Dennis finally found a permanent occupation, in the form of a civil servant, in May 1974. His main responsibility at Manpower Services was to search for employment for unskilled laborers. He was assigned to a Job Center in Denmark Street, West End, where he was given an office and – for the first time since he'd left school – he exchanged a uniform for a suit. During this time, he continued to frequent gay-friendly bars in London, including the *Pig and Whistle*, the *Black Cap*, the *Champion* in Bayswater and the infamous *Golden Lion* in Dean Street, Soho.

On a cold and rainy night in November 1975, as he came out of the *Champion*, opening his umbrella, Dennis noticed a man in his early twenties being harassed by two older men in a dark and dirty alley. The older guys didn't appear to have any weapons on them, but they were pushing the youngster around and it looked like one of them had taken the guy's wallet.

"Hey!" Dennis shouted, jogging toward them. "Leave him alone!"

Upon noticing that Dennis Nilsen was in much better physical shape than they were, the two older men dropped their hassling act and scampered away.

"Are you all right?" Dennis asked the young man upon reaching him. He shifted the umbrella in his right hand to cover both their heads.

The man looked up into his eyes and replied, "I think so. They were just messing around with me." He had blond hair in a bob, with soft facial features and faint green twinkling eyes. There were fake silver earrings in his ears and cheap pink lipstick on his lips. His brown corduroy jacket and his jeans were soaking wet.

"What's your name?" Dennis inquired.

"David," the youngster replied, extending a hand. "David Gallichan."

Dennis instantly liked him. He spoke in a soft tone and he had a friendly and honest look in his eyes. "Hello, David," he said, shaking hands. "I'm Dennis Nilsen."

David frowned. "Nilsen? Is that Norwegian?"

"Yup, though I'm actually Scottish. My biological father came from Norway but I was born in a small town called Fraserburgh in Scotland. I never really knew my real father, you know?"

"Same here," David replied, straightening his wet and dirty jacket.

Dennis stared him down and two things came to mind: judged by his clothing, David was most likely homeless, and judged by his appearance and mannerisms, he was a homosexual.

"Do you have a place to sleep tonight?" Dennis asked in a concerned tone.

David looked at down at his battered Doc Martin boots and shook his head.

"Shame, you must be cold and starving."

Lifting his head slowly, David's faint eyes twinkled again as he said, "That's the understatement of the week."

"Well, Twinkle," said Dennis, "why don't you come back to my place? I will feed you and you can borrow some of my dry clothes. What do you say about that?"

"I'd like that very much," David mumbled shyly.

They took a cab to Dennis Nilsen's room in Cricklewood, where young David Gallichan was given a dry tracksuit to wear and two cans of spaghetti and meatballs to eat.

Dennis switched on his record player and put on Queen's new album, *A night at the Opera*, starting the needle at the smash hit on side two, *Bohemian Rhapsody*. He had bought the record just a week earlier and he loved it even more than their previous album, *Sheer Heart Attack*.

Walking over to the kitchenette, he snapped his fingers to the beat of the music. "I have rum and I have beer," he told his visitor. "Which do you prefer?"

David swallowed the last bit of food and said, "A beer would be nice, thank you."

Dennis retrieved a bottle of beer from the small refrigerator in the corner of the kitchen area and handed it to David before pouring himself a strong rum and Coke.

He sat down beside David on the couch and placed a hand on his thigh. "You're unemployed aren't you, Twinkle?"

"I am looking for a job but, yes, currently I'm living on the dole. I stay at youth hostels whenever they have space available."

"Well, you can stay here just as long as you need to," Dennis offered. "At least until you get a job, that is."

David nodded thankfully. "You're a very kind man," he told Dennis. "What do you do for a living?"

"That's sort of ironic." Dennis chuckled and took a big gulp of his drink. "I'm in unemployment administration. A civil servant if you like." He reached into his jacket pocket and produced a pack of Lucky Strike cigarettes. "Smoke?" he offered.

"No, thanks," replied David.

Dennis lit up and began to tell his new friend his life story.

They spent the rest of the night listening to Queen and The Who while drinking, talking and laughing into the early hours of the morning.

The next day was a Saturday, which meant Dennis didn't have to go into the office.

After a breakfast of boiled eggs and corned beef, he fetched the newspaper from the front door and sat down on the carpet beside David. "I like you very much, Twinkle," he said. "Would you like to move into a bigger apartment with me?"

"I would love to!" David replied with sparkling eyes.

During the following few hours, they leafed through the rental advertisements in the paper and found a number of places they were interested in. That afternoon, they met with several real estate agents and went to view five or six different properties.

***

A week later, Dennis Nilsen and David Gallichan moved into a ground floor apartment at 195 Melrose Avenue, also located in Cricklewood.

Dennis used the inheritance bequeathed to him by his father to pay for the deposit and the first three months' rent. He also negotiated a deal with the friendly landlord whereby they would have exclusive use of the garden at the rear of the property.

According to the advertisement, the apartment was supposed to be fully furnished but it contained only two single beds, a kitchen table, an oil stove and three loose-standing wooden cupboards.

Over the next six months, though they were fairly poor, Nilsen and Gallichan redecorated and furnished the entire apartment with appliances, additional furniture and a larger refrigerator. The inside of the apartment also needed a lot of attention, since it was one of the older buildings in London and largely derelict. Much of this repair work was performed by David, as Dennis was putting in overtime at Manpower Services to bring in more money. David also fixed the broken fence around the backyard and made them a little veggie garden.

CHAPTER 5

The outside of their apartment at 195 Melrose Avenue was stunning, with large bay windows in the lily-white walls of the Victorian-style building, but the inside was a mess. Plaster was coming off the walls and the ceilings, the plumbing was rusty, the carpets covering the wooden floorboards were dirty, and the place smelt of mold and rotten wood.

But the couple was happy and David was making good inroads into fixing the apartment up.

On the first Saturday in December, they went to the cinema to watch a film called *Tommy: The Rock Opera*, produced by The Who, and they were both thrilled with the way it had been done. The movie was about a deaf, dumb and blind boy who became a master pinball player and, subsequently, the object of a religious cult. Dennis was now wearing his hair longer, his fringe almost touching his eyebrows, very much like The Who's songwriter and lead guitarist, Pete Townshend.

Two weeks after they had moved in, they visited a local pet shop where they bought a mongrel Collie crossbreed puppy. Instead of barking, the tiny dog only made short, high-pitched squeaks, so they decided to name her Bleep.

Although Bleep brought them closer together, Dennis never really felt that he was in love with David. It was more of a friends-with-benefits situation than an actual romantic relationship. He was now drinking more excessively every evening and on weekends he was constantly intoxicated. In this state, he often talked to himself as opposed to David.

He had showed David how to operate his 8mm film camera, but he became frustrated as David didn't listen to him and didn't appreciate the importance of good filmmaking.

As he sat in his bed without a shirt, smoking a cigarette and drinking beer from a glass, the blankets drawn up to his waist, Dennis said to

David, who was making the home video: "I can't understand you. I asked you to start filming from my feet, slowly up to my head. Don't you ever watch movies? Anybody can do it. Anybody can handle a camera, even a chimpanzee." He raised his glass and said, "Here's to you Missus Robinson."

He then swung his legs off the bed and stubbed his cigarette out in an overfull ashtray. Scratching the back of his black underpants, he looked at David with squinting eyes. "What are you doing switching the bloody thing off for? You're never going to be a cameraman, you know?" He lit another cigarette, inhaled and then rose to his feet.

"Come on, Des," mumbled David, "get rid of the underpants."

"No, no, no. I'm not going to do anything pornographic," Dennis replied, waving a dismissive hand. He took another sip of beer and raised his glass once more. "Our last London commuter," he said theatrically. "Our last tenant, being screwed by the Department of Employment, London transport, big chain stores, supermarkets..."

David didn't know what the hell Dennis was talking about – it was one of those days when he spoke to himself in incoherent sentences – but he suspected it had something to do with the Trade Union his boyfriend was so actively involved with.

"I cannot stand this beer," said Dennis, "I need to buy us a bottle of rum..." He looked away and added, "Okay, cut now. Let me think."

An hour later, he was dressed in a white shirt with a navy jacket and formal trousers. David was filming him while he was playing with Bleep on the carpet. "Check that bloody dog," Dennis remarked. "It chewed my slippers again. I'll wring its bloody neck when I catch it doing that again."

He knelt beside one of the beds and shoved pieces of plaster from the blankets onto the floor, before standing up and walking over to the French doors leading to the backyard. "So, this is what happened last night," he announced to the camera. "My drink was over there." He pointed at the bed in the corner of the room. "Me over here... Move the camera up there, Twinkle."

David focused the camera on a large hole in the ceiling.

"Just look at that," Dennis continued his monologue. "The whole bloody ceiling fell down. It fell down on me for a start, then it hit the dog." He crouched to pick up two brick-sized concrete fragments and said, while dragging on his cigarette, "Big chunks of masonry. It could kill somebody." Then he dropped the pieces of concrete to the floor. "Look at that!"

Little did Dennis Nilsen know that this rare video footage would go viral on the Internet a decade or two later.

Three months after they had moved in together, Dennis came home to find David on the bed, playing with a stray tabby cat.

"And who might this be?" he asked, stroking the animal's grey-striped coat.

"Hi, Des," David said hesitantly. "She just came here this morning, so I fed her and now she's not going away. I think we'll have to keep her."

Dennis raised his eyebrows. "What about Bleep? Isn't she going to fight with the cat?"

David stared at Bleep, where she was curled up on a couch, sleeping. "They are the best of friends," he told Dennis with a smile on his face. "Bleep licked the cat's nose this morning and they shared food from the same bowl without any animosity."

"All right then," replied Dennis. He took off his jacket and tie and draped them over one of the leather armchairs he had bought with his previous paycheck. Sitting down next to David and the cat on the bed, he asked, "What shall we call her?"

"I was thinking Dee-Dee." David looked down at the cat and pressed his index finger on its forehead. "You are a Dee-Dee, aren't you?"

"Why Dee-Dee?" asked Dennis.

David squinted. "Don't you get it? D for David and D for Dennis: Dee-Dee."

Dennis laughed.

That was the last time he would laugh in a very long time.

After Dee-Dee's arrival, things started going downhill for them as a couple.

Nothing came of David Gallichan's promises to search for a job; he showed a lack of any employment ambitions whatsoever. Dennis began to view himself as the breadwinner in the house and it seemed like David didn't appreciate it. He kept on brining strangers to the apartment and the frequency of the couple's sexual intercourse diminished rapidly. While Dennis stayed at home in the evenings, drinking alone, David went out to the gay pubs and had multiple affairs with other men.

Their superficial relationship continued to decline over the following fifteen months and they began to argue over almost everything under the sun.

The final fight took place in the summer of 1978.

David was complaining about how Dennis was always working and that the two of them were never spending time together anymore.

"Well, one of us has to work!" Dennis shouted, throwing a frying pan into the kitchen basin. "Where else do you think our bloody money is going to come from?"

"It's all about money with you, you selfish bitch!" David retorted. "You just want me to be dependent on you, that's all you've ever wanted."

Dennis clenched his jaw and balled his fists. "Fuck you, Twinkle! You are such a tart. You are always screwing around with other guys and I am sick and tired of it!"

"I can leave if you want me to! Is that what you want, Des?"

In that moment of anger, Dennis Nilsen made a mistake he would later regret deeply by saying, "Pack your bags, David Gallichan, you're out of here."

BONFIRE BODIES

David packed up his belongings and left for good.

CHAPTER 6

The last six months of 1978 proved to be a dark time for Dennis Nilsen.

David's abandonment caused him to slide into a constant drinking binge and his life was spiralling out of control. He fell into a rut of work, drink, have sex, sleep, and then repeat.

Dee-Dee had run away after David left, so Dennis and Bleep were the only two permanent occupants left in the apartment on Melrose Avenue.

Other than drinking rum and Coca Cola alone at home, Nilsen's remaining three affections were cooking food, listening to music and caring for Bleep. When he arrived home in the evenings, he would feed and brush Bleep before pouring drink after drink, while listening to music in the lounge or cooking up a storm in the kitchen.

In the beginning, during the first two months after David had left, Dennis would make treats in the evenings and take it to work for his colleagues to taste the next day. His colleagues enjoyed these tasting sessions, especially when Dennis made one of his curry dishes.

But when this habit eventually died, he only had Bleep and his music. He would bathe Bleep every weekend and take her for long walks on Hampstead Heath, one of London's most popular parks, not too far from Trafalgar Square. During these walks, he often took his 8mm camera with and filmed young men walking around or having lunch in the park.

Bleep became his only companion and Dennis Nilsen believed that (other than his grandfather all those years ago) the Collie was the only living creature who ever truly loved him. His soul felt defeated and the loneliness was strangling his emotions into a dark place, reminding him of that day when he nearly drowned in Aberdeenshire.

He would roam the gay pubs in London on Friday and Saturday nights, picking up slim and attractive (and vulnerable) young men, luring them back to his apartment for drinks, food, warmth and sex. Some of these men came back for a second and even a third time, but when they finally realized that Dennis Nilsen was nothing but a miserable drunk, boozing away his sorrows, they also abandoned him the way David had done.

Dennis was missing David Gallichan's company tremendously but he could not for the life of him get another long-term relationship going with anyone. He started thinking that he had just become an impossible person to live with.

During the fall of 1978, when the pub scene became less vibrant, he mostly stayed at home and drank on his own in the evenings. He also resumed his Yemen fetish of masturbating in front of a mirror, mostly when he was intoxicated. Dennis would use heavy make-up to darken his eyes, whiten his face, and color his lips in purple – creating the illusion of a corpse – then masturbate while staring at his reflection in the mirror, pretending he was having sexual intercourse with a lifeless body.

By late 1978, at the age of thirty-three, he was living a near solitary existence.

Although his drinking was affecting his attendance record at the office, he often volunteered to work overtime and his colleagues and superiors still regarded him as a trustworthy employee who was devoted to the cause of fighting unemployment. His job at Manpower Services also allowed him to study the behavior of London's unemployed male population, a vulnerable society of young men, more closely.

Dennis was a staunch Labor supporter and a fierce union negotiator, and he started devoting an increasing amount of his time and effort to his work, in a frantic attempt to pull his life together.

But the bottle hindered this endeavour.

His craving for alcohol, whether it was beer, rum or whiskey, made him become delusional and paranoid as he drank himself into a stupor on many nights.

CHAPTER 7

On the evening of December 30th, 1978, Dennis Nilsen was feeling exceptionally frisky, for the first time in months. He had polished three double rum and Cokes alone in his apartment and he was craving homosexual companionship.

The atmosphere in London was electric in anticipation of New Year's Eve. Thousands of tourists were roaming the streets and loud music sounded from the pubs and nightclubs.

Dennis made sure Bleep had enough food and water, then went outside and locked the door behind him. It was cold but not yet snowing. He walked a few blocks up Melrose Avenue until he reached *Cricklewood Arms*, the closest pub to his apartment. He was in high spirits when he entered the establishment. He was going to score tonight, all right.

It was still early and there were not many patrons inside the warm and cosy pub. A wood fire crackled in the fireplace and the aroma of pipe tobacco hung in the air. Dennis sat down on one of the barstools at the mahogany bar counter and ordered a beer, gazing around at the handful of people inside. He was still wearing his work attire, although he had taken off his tie earlier.

He was just about to engage in small talk with the bartender, when an attractive young man with bright blue eyes and curly brown hair walked into the pub. He crossed the floor and came to a halt right beside Dennis. Then he pulled a wad of notes from his back pocket and said to the bartender, in a heavy Irish accent, "One draught beer and one shot of Scotch, please?"

Dennis estimated the young lad to be about seventeen or eighteen years of age. What he did not know at the time was that this boy was still a few months shy of his fifteenth birthday. His name was Stephen Holmes and as an early bloomer he was just past puberty.

"Can I see some I.D?" asked the bartender, a skinhead in his mid-twenties.

"Don't have it on me," the young lad replied nonchalantly.

The bartender shook his head. "Then I can't serve you. Sorry, fella."

"Come on now," Dennis Nilsen protested. "Give the young man a break. It's the holiday season for Pete's sake." He turned to face the lad and asked, "What's your name?"

"Stephen," came the reply.

Dennis lit a cigarette and glared at the skinhead behind the bar. "By the looks of it, Stephen over here is about eighteen, so what do you say mister bartender?"

"Nah," replied the bartender, "he doesn't look a day older than sixteen to me."

Dennis returned his gaze to Stephen. "How old are you?" he asked.

"What's it to you?" Stephen said irritably.

"Look, I'm only trying to help, okay?" Dennis told him. He was impressed by Stephen's feisty attitude and he could already feel an erection developing in the warmth of his crotch.

Stephen shoved the notes back into his pocket and said to the bartender, "Nevermind. I'll buy my booze somewhere else if you don't want the business."

The skinhead bartender snorted and then attended to two newcomers on the other side of the counter.

Stephen was about to turn and leave when Dennis grabbed his arm. "Wait," he pleaded, dragging on his cigarette. "Come sit down, I have a proposition for you." He inhaled smoke, blew it out through his nose and then stubbed the cigarette out in a porcelain ashtray.

When the boy hesitantly sat down next to him, Dennis held out his hand and said, "My name is Dennis, but you can call me Des, okay?"

Shaking his hand, Stephen gave a shy nod. "What's the proposition?" he asked, rubbing his slender hands over his knees and thighs.

Dennis folded his arms across his chest. "Well, it seems like you have a dilemma, young Stephen. Now, I don't know how old you are and I don't really care. However, I like your attitude and if you are willing to come back to my place down the road to keep me company, I will give you some rum and Coke to drink. I have a shitload of the stuff."

Stephen's face grew radiant. "I love rum and Coke!" he said excitedly.

"Shhh," Dennis cautioned him with a finger to his lips. "We do not want any of the other people to know about our plans now, do we?"

Let's get out of here you sexy little thing, he thought as he placed a one Pound bill next to his half-finished beer on the bar counter, while he slowly rose to his feet. He was excited and anxious at the same time. Without saying another word, he made his way toward the door and then gave a satisfying nod as he noticed, in his peripheral vision, that Stephen was following him.

They reached his apartment in just over five minutes and Dennis allowed the boy to walk in first. When Dennis switched on the lights, Bleep made a squeaking sound and ran toward the door.

"Aah, he's so cute." Stephen said in a small voice. "What's his name?"

Dennis closed the door and replied, "It's a she. Her name is Bleep. Go on, pick her up."

Stephen carefully picked the dog up and settled in one of the armchairs, cuddling Bleep on his lap.

"What sort of music do you usually listen to?" asked Dennis. He studied the boy's lean legs in his stovepipe jeans and his mouth was watering.

"Oh, rock music, mostly," Stephen answered.

Walking over to the record player on a small table against the wall, Dennis chose The Who's album, *Quadrophenia*, before pouring them each a stiff rum and Coke.

He sat down across from Stephen and they began chatting away like old friends.

Dennis, who didn't want to scare the youth away, didn't make a sexual move until very late that night. The problem he faced then was that they were both so drunk they could barely stand up straight. He wanted to screw the boy's brains out but he simply couldn't get an erection.

Instead, they undressed while laughing and stumbling around, and finally got into bed together where they fell asleep within minutes.

***

The next morning, Dennis woke up just after seven o'clock with a headache straight from the devil's breath. Stephen Holmes was still sleeping beside him in the bed, naked.

After gulping down two aspirin tablets he'd found in the bedside table's drawer, Dennis stared at the sleeping boy and then he suddenly broke out in a cold sweat. *What if I wake him up and he wants to leave?* his thoughts began to stir inside. *I don't want him to leave, we had such a great time last night.*

His red-and-white striped tie was still hanging around the bedpost where he'd left it the previous day. When he noticed the formal neck tie, it struck him that he did not have to go to work. It was New Year's Eve and the offices of Manpower Services were closed for the day.

Dennis slowly pulled the tie down, thinking, *I want to celebrate the new year with you, young Stephen, whether you want me to or not.* He desperately did not want the boy to leave like David and all his other one-night stands had done.

Stephen was on his stomach, with his head facing the other way, snoring lightly. Dennis slowly sat upright and tried to control his breathing. He used his right hand to slip the thin end of the tie underneath the boy's throat, careful not to wake him, and then he pulled it upward with his left hand on the other side. Stephen stirred briefly as the polyester fabric of the tie grazed his Adams apple but then he was still again.

Holding the two ends of the tie in his hands, Dennis tightened his grip and began to pull and squeeze. Stephen Holmes awoke from the immense pressure around his neck but the only sound he was able to make was muffled gurgle.

Dennis straddled him and planted his knees firmly into the boy's back, as his hands and feet violently swayed around. Dennis squeezed tighter for another two minutes, while Stephen made more gurgling and snorting noises, before the body became limp beneath Dennis Nilsen's knees.

The adrenalin rush of total control and domination flooded through Nilsen's veins like spring tide on Philorth Beach. He was caught by surprize when he realized his own strength. Letting go of the tie, he threw his head back, panting for air. The sensation was thrilling.

Upon noticing that Stephen was still breathing, but now unconscious, Dennis got up and walked to the kitchen area to fetch the medium-sized plastic bucket he always used to bathe Bleep in. Bleep was still fast asleep under the kitchen table. He filled the bucket with cold water and returned to the bed where his victim lay motionless.

He placed the bucket on the floor and then re-positioned Stephen's body in order to submerge his head in the water. Dennis grabbed him by the hair and pushed his head down, waiting for the small bubbles drifting to the surface to disappear. The fourteen-year-old boy's body convulsed for another minute and then, just like that, life was drained from him forever.

Dennis Nilsen's heart was hammering against his ribcage and his mind was swimming in a sea of dead bodies; he saw his dead grandfather, corpses of soldiers in Yemen, the naked deceased man in *The Raft of the Medusa* painting and, finally, the nude body of young Stephen Holmes, the legs still on the bed and the torso now hanging over into the bucket of water.

As brief sense of regret washed over Dennis as he stood back and looked at what he had done. Then he pulled himself together and hissed through gritted teeth, "Let's see if you can leave my apartment now, you son of a bitch." He left the body in that awkward position, pulled on a pair of jeans and an olive green woollen jersey, then went back to the kitchen to make some coffee to calm his nerves.

After drinking a cup of coffee and smoking three cigarettes in succession, Dennis took Bleep out into the garden and then returned to Stephen's corpse by the bed, an hour after the boy had taken his last breath.

He gradually arranged the body into a horizontal position, upside down across the bed, and spread its legs. By now, he was sexually aroused beyond logical reasoning.

When he bent down and fondled the boy's soft testicles, covered in fluffy brown hair, Dennis Nilsen's erection was pressing so hard against his jeans that it hurt.

Ripping off the jeans, he straddled the body and pushed his penis between the deceased boy's firm buttocks. It took him nine seconds of sliding back and forth over the crevice before he reached a massive orgasm, shooting a stream of semen all over the back of the corpse.

He rolled off the body and collapsed onto the bed in utter satisfaction. A dreamy smile formed on Nilsen's lips as he slowly closed his eyes.

He was at a turning point in his life.

There was no going back now…

CHAPTER 8

"Let's get you cleaned up, Sweetie," Dennis told the corpse on his bed three hours later. He had fallen asleep beside the body and it was now nearly eleven o'clock in the morning.

He rose to his feet, then hoisted the boy's body to his shoulders and carried it to the bathroom.

After placing the limp body on the tiled bathroom floor, Dennis ran a hot bath while sitting on the side of the bathtub, thinking about what to do next. He was once again surprized by his ability to remain calm in such a dire situation. The thought had crossed his mind to turn himself in to the police, but he now decided he would first wait to see if anybody reported Stephen missing.

The bath was ready and Dennis clumsily dunked the dead body into the water.

He was still dressed only in his jersey and when the naked corpse grazed against his penis, as he pushed it into the tub, he could feel his erection returning. However, Dennis focussed his mind on the task at hand and his sexual organ soon returned to its floppy state. He washed the body meticulously, starting at the feet and working his way up until he had shampooed the hair and wiped the pale face with a washcloth. He briefly considered shaving the chin, but discarded the idea upon noticing how fluffy the facial hair was. Dennis was beginning to wonder whether the boy had perhaps been a number of years younger than eighteen while he was still alive.

When the corpse was clean enough to his liking, Dennis Nilsen placed a towel on the floor and then struggled to lift the body out of the tub and onto the towel.

After drying Stephen's cadaver with a second towel, Dennis walked to the lounge to fetch the boy's jeans and his shirt. Upon returning to the bathroom, he propped the body up against the bathtub and said,

"Come on, Darling, let's get you dressed. I think it's going to be a cold day."

He battled to get the legs into the jeans but the shirt was easier. When he was finished, Nilsen carried the corpse back to the bed and tucked it in, the way a mother would do to her child before bedtime. Then he put on his pyjama pants and sat down on the edge of the bed, shaking his head slightly.

"Bleep?" he called nervously.

His gaze swept the room and then he remembered that the dog was still outside.

Once he had let Bleep back in, Dennis poured himself a hefty rum – with a dash of Coke to take the edge off – and drank deeply from the glass. He switched on his small portable radio beside the television, sat down in an armchair and waited for the next news report.

From where he was sitting, he could see the bed with the dead body under the covers, and he now noticed that the feet of the corpse were sticking out and that Bleep was licking the toes.

"Bleep!" he yelled, jumping up from the chair. "This has got nothing to do with you. Out!" He opened the doors to the backyard and chased the dog outside.

"Sorry about that, Stevie," Dennis said to the cadaver upon easing the doors shut behind him again. He covered the feet with one of his jackets before resuming his television channel search.

It was now well past noon and there was nothing about a missing Stephen Holmes on any of the news flashes. Not even a mention of an unidentified missing young man.

Dennis nodded his head in satisfaction.

This confirmed his suspicion that Stevie had been homeless. Not staying in youth hostels or shelters; properly homeless, sleeping in the streets of London.

He decided to spend New Year's Eve with Stevie and then get rid of the body in the morning.

How do I get rid of the body? he thought to himself.

This was a predicament that had been brooding in the back of his mind ever since he'd put Stevie's corpse in the bed. He couldn't drive somewhere to dump it because he didn't own a motor vehicle. Hell, he didn't even have a driver's license! Whenever he had to go somewhere, he either walked or made use of cabs and the underground tube.

Without any solution springing to mind, Dennis stood up and went to the kitchen area to fix himself something to eat. His hangover had subsided to such an extent that his stomach could now handle solids. All the curtains were still drawn – not allowing the weak winter sun into the apartment – so he switched on the dim kitchen light and made himself a ham and tomato sandwich.

After wolfing down the sandwich, he smoked another two Lucky Strike cigarettes while pacing up and down in the lounge. *Everything is going to be okay*, his subconscious told him in a remarkably relaxed tone.

Later, Dennis Nilsen would tell the police that he had no recollection of spending the day in his apartment while a deceased young boy lay in his bed.

He spent the rest of the afternoon drinking rum and having conversations with himself about the disposal of the body. When darkness came at half-past-five, he had finished the bottle of rum (with a few shots of whiskey chasers in-between) and he was finally intoxicated enough to go back to sleep. Although in a drunken haze, Dennis still had the presence of mind to allow poor Bleep back into the apartment and to lock the doors.

He removed his pants, climbed into the bed with the corpse and then undressed it. But he was too inebriated to get an erection, so Dennis played with the dead body's limp private parts until he fell asleep just after seven o'clock on New Year's Eve.

***

The following morning, he celebrated the first day of 1979 by simulating sex and ejaculating over the corpse again.

Dennis rolled the body onto him, in a missionary position, and then began to thrust his erect penis between the stiff inner thighs of the legs that were now affected by severe rigor mortis. Like the morning before, he reached an orgasm within seconds but this time he didn't fall asleep afterwards. He pushed the cold carcass off his torso as a feeling of disgust suddenly washed over him. He knew that it was dysfunctional to be attracted to the deceased boy, but he simply could not help himself.

Getting up, he rubbed his eyes with his fists and yawned before stretching his arms above his head. Then he froze as his gaze locked on a broken floorboard, sticking out from underneath the dirty carpet. While he kept on staring at the floorboard, where it met the skirting against the southern wall of the lounge, an idea popped into Dennis Nilsen's mind. An idea that would allow him to quickly solve his predicament without drawing any attention from outsiders.

After wiping his semen from the legs of the corpse with a paper towel, Nilsen moved the chairs and couches to the kitchen area and rolled up the carpet in the lounge. Then he lifted three of the floorboards with a chisel he had found in David Gallichan's forgotten "renovation trunk" under the bed.

The ground beneath the floorboards was clammy and covered in hundreds of cobwebs, but he was glad to learn that the eighteen inches between the floorboards and the earth's soil was more than enough to conceal his dead flatmate.

Dennis dragged the stiff body over to the hole in the floor and carefully slid it into the space beneath the boards. To his relief, Bleep didn't wake up from the noise he was making. The last thing he wanted was for the dog to be sniffing around or licking the corpse again.

After crossing Stephen's hands over his chest – the way Grandpa had been buried – Dennis put the floorboards back in place and covered it with the carpet, thinking: *Now we will be together forever.*

When he was done, he took a deep breath, then stood back and dusted off his hands. "Sweet dreams, Stevie," he muttered before hauling the few pieces of furniture back into the lounge. Then he made a small fire in the backyard and burned Stephen's clothing to ashes.

The ease of the tasks he had just completed astonished Dennis Nilsen. He had swiftly disposed of a dead body without taking any risk whatsoever. Nobody would ever know his secret.

As a reward for his brilliant thinking, he poured himself another glass of rum – this time without the Coke.

It was 9:12 a.m in the morning.

CHAPTER 9

A week after he had buried the cadaver beneath the floorboards, he became curious and started wondering whether decomposition had begun.

Poor Stevie, he thought. *I need to check on you; make sure you're all right.*

He exhumed the body that evening and was surprized to learn that, other than being extremely dirty, it was still very much intact. The skin had turned from ivory to a blueish grey and the flesh was bloated, but it still looked like a human being and there was no strange odor coming from it.

After Dennis had undressed himself, he hugged the cold body of Stephen Holmes and then carried it to the bathroom for another hot bath. By now, he regarded the corpse as one of his valued possessions and he had always taken great care of his possessions. He bathed the body with the same nurture as a week before, then clipped its fingernails and powdered its face.

When he buried the carcass the second time, he didn't want it to become dirt-stained again so he wrapped it in dustbin liners before sliding it back into the opening underneath the floorboards.

Following the second burial, Dennis continued to live his life as if nothing had ever happened.

He went to work every day and returned home in the evenings, knowing that there was a corpse beneath his apartment floor. To the rational brain this might have seemed absurd, but to Dennis it was the most natural thing in the world. He finally had the company he'd been searching for, ever since he had left the army, right under his feet.

Furthermore, things were going very well at work. By the spring of 1979 – two days after the Iron Lady, Margaret Thatcher, was sworn in as Prime Minister of the United Kingdom – Dennis Nilsen was appointed Acting Executive Officer at Manpower Services in Denmark Street.

During this same time period, his eyesight began to deteriorate from all the administrative labor and an optometrist issued him with a prescription for reading glasses. Dennis purchased his steel-rimmed eyeglasses from a pharmacy not far from his apartment and soon started wearing them permanently because he thought it made him appear more sophisticated.

By the end of an unusually hot London summer – seven months after he had stashed the body beneath the floorboards – the foul stench of decaying flesh began to fill the apartment. Bleep was becoming restless and Dennis wore a scarf over his mouth and nose on most evenings. The place was beginning to smell like a drain clogged with rotten meat.

He knew he had to make another plan. He had to get rid of the deathly odor somehow.

On the second Saturday in August, Dennis went outside and made a big bonfire in the garden behind his apartment. The walls around the backyard were quite high, so while his neighbors would see the smoke, they wouldn't be able to figure out *what* was burning. As the fire was gaining momentum, Dennis exhumed the body from beneath the floorboards in the lounge once again and dragged it across the apartment floor, up to the French doors.

Upon smelling the unearthly stench of young Stephen's decomposing corpse, Nilsen realized he had to find a way to disguise the smell it was going to emit once it was burning. Walking out into the yard, he instantly found the solution. When David had still been living there, he had created a row of flower beds in half a dozen car tyres, filling the inside of the tires with soil and seeds.

Dennis emptied the dirt from one of these tyres and chucked it onto the bonfire before adding the dead body of Stephen Holmes. A sense of peace filled him when he said, "Have a good afterlife, Stevie. May you never encounter someone as evil as me wherever you're going next."

He lit a cigarette as he sat down in the garden and watched black smoke rise up from the bonfire. Sniffing the air, a smile played across Dennis Nilsen's lips.

His plan with the tyre had worked; the smell of the smouldering rubber was so overwhelming, he couldn't even detect a whiff of burning flesh.

What he didn't know at the time, was that within four months, the craving for company would gnaw at his soul and cause him to search for a new deceased flatmate. Exhuming and burning Stephen's body would leave a void in his heart and an empty hole beneath his apartment.

He was alone again.

CHAPTER 10

Monday, December 3rd, 1979 started with the same routine as any working day for Dennis.

He woke up at 6:30 a.m. with the usual hangover from the previous night's drinking. After taking two aspirin tablets, he dressed in his suit and then took Bleep out for her morning business before grabbing his overcoat and stepping out into a rare sunshiny day in London's winter.

As the Acting Executive Officer at Manpower Services, Dennis Nilsen now had much more freedom with his office hours and, after a long and quiet morning's work, he decided to take an early lunch at one of West End's pubs.

Walking down Denmark Street with his spirits high, he admired the effort that the city council had put into this year's early Christmas decorations. The buildings around him all had strings of red, white, green, gold and silver decorations hanging from them, with mistletoe rings above the doors of some of the stores. He passed *Hank's Acoustics*, *Wunjo Guitars* and *Constantinou Hairstylists* before crossing Tottenham Court Road and reaching the old English pub he sometimes frequented at lunchtime. The sun was still shining, but it was exceptionally cold outside and the weather forecast had predicted snow for later in the week.

Dennis entered the cosy pub and settled in his usual spot at the bar counter after he had removed his coat and jacket. He placed his order and two minutes later the bartender brought him a pint of Guinness; a drink he had come to love in winter, especially during the day. Evenings were reserved for rum and Coke.

There was an attractive man in his early twenties, studying a street map of London, two barstools away from Dennis. His golden-brown hair was longer than most men and he had a feminine mouth that appeared to be smiling even though he was deep in thought. He was wearing a blue tracksuit and an expensive-looking camera was hanging from a nylon strap around his shoulder.

Moving to the barstool next to the man, Dennis said, "You not from around here?"

The young man flinched and looked up from the battered map. "Huh?" he replied. "I'm sorry, you startled me there."

"Are you a tourist or something?" Dennis asked.

"Sort of," the man replied, extending a hand. "Kenneth. Kenneth Ockenden."

Dennis shook his hand. "Nice to meet you Kenneth. I'm Dennis Nilsen." He frowned and took a sip of his beer. "Ockenden? Are you from up north? Norway? Sweden?"

Kenneth chuckled. "No, actually I'm all the way from Canada. I'm a student there."

"So, Mr Canadian, what brings you to this part of the world?" Dennis asked, peering over the rim of his glasses. He offered Kenneth a cigarette while lighting one for himself.

Declining the cigarette, Kenneth pointed at the map and said, "I visited some relatives in Carshalton, after touring the Lake District in the northwest last week, and now I am making a quick stop in Central London before I'm going back to Canada for Christmas with my parents."

Dennis puffed on his smoke. "I see," he said, nodding. "Well, you are speaking to the right man, Ken. I know this shithole of a city like the back of my hand. No need for that map."

"Really?" Kenneth said. His eyes lit up. "I've never been here in my life. I mean, I saw Big Ben from afar earlier but other than that I don't know any of the tourist attractions."

They chatted about the city for another hour, ordering one more round of beer, and then Dennis glanced at his wristwatch. "Well, it's almost three o'clock," he mentioned, shrugging his shoulders. "It will be a waste of time for me to return to the office now. What do you say I take you on a quick tour of Central London, young lad?"

"That would be wonderful," replied Kenneth. "Tell me something: what do you do for a living anyway? You seem to know an awful lot about the city's administration."

"Oh, I'm a civil servant," Dennis told him. "I work in the unemployment sector. A rather boring job I have to say. I fill out forms and stamp them, then I fill out more forms and stamp them, too."

Kenneth Ockenden laughed and finished his beer. "Let's go then!" he said excitedly.

Dennis took him to Trafalgar Square and Piccadilly Circus, then to Westminster Abby and finally to the Westminster Palace and Big Ben. The Canadian student was overjoyed that it was such a clear day. He used up three rolls of film while taking photographs at all the different landmarks.

When they returned early in the evening, Dennis suggested that Kenneth join him for supper at his apartment. He had determined that Ockenden wasn't gay, but he could use the company just the same.

"I'll tell you some more about the history of London," he said, "and I have a superb record collection. We can listen to music and perhaps go out for another drink later."

Kenneth agreed with the suggestion and went with Dennis to the apartment at 195 Melrose Avenue in Cricklewood. He enjoyed the older man's wisdom and he had been hanging onto his lips the entire afternoon during their sightseeing trip.

Bleep instantly liked Kenneth Ockenden and sat on his lap at the kitchen table while Dennis was in front of the stove, cooking.

"So, I see you guys have a female Prime Minister now," Kenneth commented, stroking Bleep's fur. "What do you think of her?"

"I like her, Ken," replied Dennis. "I think she is going to be staunch and she will sort out Britain's fiscal problems. She's already talking about introducing a series of economic policies intended to reverse the high unemployment figures."

"Fair enough, but will she have the balls to implement them?"

"That woman has bigger balls than yours and mine together," Dennis replied, and they both laughed.

"That smells delicious. What are you making?"

Dennis smiled. "It's a surprize. I hope you're hungry.

"Starving," said Kenneth Ockenden, returning the smile.

***

After they had enjoyed a light supper of an egg quiche with ham and fries, the two men changed their minds about going out for drinks. Instead, they bought whiskey, rum and beer at an off-license near the Willesden Green underground station and returned to the apartment for their own little party.

They drank as if it were the last day on earth and Dennis put on record after record, playing Queen, Led Zeppelin and The Who until late after midnight.

"When are you going back to Canada, Kenny?" he asked in the early hours of the morning. His voice was slurring and his mind foggy.

Kenneth swayed his head back and forth and slurred back, "Tomorrow night."

That sent a shock through Dennis Nilsen's system. The fogginess was instantly gone from his mind. *Tomorrow? No, no you can't! I'm just getting to know you. You can't go away tomorrow, Kenny. You have to stay here with me, damn it!*

"That's a pity," he told Kenneth. "I was just beginning to enjoy your company."

"Same here," Ockenden replied, a tone of sincerity in his drunken voice.

Dennis put on The Who's latest album, *Who are you?* and skipped the needle to track four on side one: *Sister Disco*. "Listen, Kenny," he said, "this song's stereo is amazing, but you have to listen to it through the headphones." They were sitting on the carpet in front of the record player and Dennis handed his visitor the headphones after plugging it in.

Kenneth placed the headphones over his ears and began to hum to the tune of the music.

The anger about the Canadian student's return to his home country now boiling inside Dennis Nilsen, he rose to his unsteady feet, grabbed the cord of the headphones and began to strangle Kenneth with it. Nilsen's face turned red as he pulled tighter and tighter, shouting, "Give me back the headphones, Kenny! I also want to listen to the song!" Kenneth Ockenden didn't struggle. He couldn't struggle; he was too sloshed. Dennis was now dragging him around on the apartment's floor, the cord digging into the young man's throat like a vice grip.

He was dead within four minutes.

Dennis Nilsen had killed a second man.

This time he didn't need the bucket of water to drown his victim in. The man was dead, all right.

Untangling the cord from Ockenden's neck, Dennis plugged the headphones in again, poured himself another rum and listened to the remaining songs on side one. Then he turned the record over to side two and listened to all those tracks as well, all while sipping on his rum. When his glass was empty, he followed the same ritual he'd performed on Stephen Holmes: he bathed the body, put it in his bed and fondled the private parts until he fell asleep...

The following morning, Dennis had to go to work so he shoved the body into a cupboard and made sure Bleep had enough food and water before leaving. On his way out, he noticed Kenneth's camera, which was still on the kitchen table, and his mind drifted back to his army days when he had photographed his fellow soldiers while they played dead. All of a sudden, he was excited. Now he had a real dead man to photograph. He picked up the camera but then sighed and ran a hand through his hair when he realized that the film was full.

Dennis went to work like any other day and returned to his apartment at five o'clock that afternoon. On his way back from the office, he stopped at a small supermarket to buy a cheap Polaroid camera. That way, he reasoned, he would not have to explain anything to anyone developing the photos afterwards.

Back in his apartment, he retrieved Ockenden's corpse from the cupboard and began to take photographs of the body in various suggestive positions. He was impressed by the clarity in which the Polaroids depicted the cadaver's beautiful features.

He then dressed the body in Kenneth Ockenden's tracksuit and propped it up on an armchair in front of the television. After pouring himself another proper rum and Coke, he seated himself alongside the corpse and switched on the television.

The story was all over the six o'clock news:

...and in international news, a student from Canada went missing in London between yesterday and today, after he had been visiting England for a tour of three weeks. 23-year-old Kenneth Ockenden was last seen in the Southampton area two days ago, before he travelled to London by train. His parents became suspicious when they didn't hear anything from their son in over 24 hours. Ockenden was supposed to check in to a flight from London to Ontario at five o'clock this afternoon. If anyone has seen this man, please contact Scotland Yard on 20 7230 1212...

A black-and-white headshot photo of Kenneth was displayed on the television screen.

"Holy crap, Kenny!" Dennis Nilsen exclaimed, staring at the dead body beside him. "Look at that! They are searching for you, dude."

Realizing that someone might have spotted them together at one of the tourist attractions the previous day, Nilsen went into a slight panic attack; not because he had any remorse in taking Ockenden's life, but because he was shit-scared of going to prison.

He thought the dilemma through and then dismissed his fear. *If push comes to shove, I will just burn the body on a bonfire like I did with Stevie.*

After watching television for another forty-five minutes, he got up and undressed the body before carefully wrapping it in plastic dustbin liner bags. Then he stowed the Kenneth Ockenden corpse beneath the floorboards, in the exact same spot where the body of Stephen Holmes had been lying for seven months.

***

Over the following two weeks, Dennis masturbated twice a day, drooling over the disgusting Polaroid photos displaying Kenneth's deceased body.

On four occasions the sensation wasn't vivid enough, so he disinterred Kenneth Ockenden's body to masturbate and ejaculate over the naked corpse. Afterwards, he would wash the cadaver, dress it in his pyjamas and seat it upon an armchair alongside him. He would watch television, drink rum and have conversations with the dead body for several hours before stowing it back in its "bed" below the floorboards in the lounge.

He would watch episodes of the television series *CHIPs* with Ockenden's corpse beside him and comment on the character Frank Poncherello's body by saying, "What do you think of that hottie, Ken? I think he is sexy, but not nearly as sexy as you."

Dennis Nilsen never expected any answers from the cadaver, however, he enjoyed every minute of these "conversations" with his macabre companion.

One evening, when Margaret Thatcher was giving one of her famous "set this nation back on the road to recovery" speeches, Dennis pointed at the television while looking at the corpse beside him.

"What did I tell you, Kenny?" he exclaimed. "Listen to that woman. She's got bigger balls than both of ours together. Bugger me!" Bleep was sitting in the corner minding her own business, as if the dead body wasn't even in the room.

Before he went to bed, following these television sessions, Nilsen would undress the body again and wrap it in plastic bags before burying it beneath the floorboards.

"Good night, Kenneth," he would politely tell the corpse every time. It was a nice flatmate to have; it was silent, still and passive, unlike Twinkle had been.

After Nilsen had exhumed Ockenden's body for the fourth time, it was starting to give off a sour odor, so he ceased their television chats.

Pretending to have the flu, he didn't go to work from December 18th until Christmas Eve, and after that he was on annual leave until the next year. Dennis Nilsen nearly drank himself to death during these two weeks. For the first time he understood that he had a sick mind and needed help. Except the help he sought did not sit in the white office of a psychiatrist, it came in a bottle.

He spent New Year's Eve 1979 alone in his apartment and slept into the new decade in a drunk muddle.

CHAPTER 11

On Friday, May 16th, 1980, a week after the slasher horror film *Friday the 13th* was released in cinemas, Dennis Nilsen had to attend a Labor Union conference in Southport, a seaside town in Merseyside, about two hundred miles north of London.

The conference stretched over two days and he slept over in a fancy hotel in Southport that evening. Due to the magnitude of the conference, there were many young men in the hotel's bar (some gay and some straight) and Nilsen had a marvellous time chatting to them, exchanging army stories and praising the work of the Iron Lady, who was actively combatting unemployment in Great Britain. The problem was that this social interaction stirred something inside him for the first time since he had killed Kenneth Ockenden.

The next day, after the morning's conference session, Dennis took the train from Southport back to London at two o'clock in the afternoon. Spring was in the air and he was feeling frisky again, like on the day that he'd met Stephen Holmes in the *Cricklewood Arms*.

During the three-hour train trip, Dennis was reading *The Dead Zone* by Stephen King and he smiled to himself a number of times when he thought of the space beneath the floorboards of 195 Melrose Avenue as his own dead zone.

The train arrived at Euston railway station, the southern terminus of the West Coast Main Line, shortly after five o'clock that Saturday afternoon. It was still light outside and a slight breeze was blowing over the concrete platform. Dennis tucked his tiny overnight suitcase under his arm and made his way to the exit.

As he walked out onto Euston square, he noticed a youth begging for money next to the trolley station. "Please, sir," the boy said in a trembling voice. "Do you perhaps have a Pound to spare for a bread and a carton of milk? I haven't eaten in days."

Dennis believed the teenager. He was skinny and shivering – despite the mild spring temperature – and his clothes were unbelievably filthy. His curly brown hair was ruffled and he had bewildered eyes with dimples in his cheeks.

"What is your name, lad?" he asked the boy.

"Martyn Duffey, sir," the youth replied, rising to his feet. He rubbed his hands together and shuffled around on the concrete floor.

"Please stop calling me sir," Dennis Nilsen told him. "How old are you, Mr Duffey?"

The lad licked his dry lips, then said, "I'm sixteen, sir."

Giving up on the "sir" lecturing, Nilsen placed a hand on Duffey's shoulder and spoke in a soft tone. "Martyn, do you have a place where you can overnight?"

"N-no, s-sir," Martyn Duffey stuttered.

"Then come with me," Dennis instructed. "Let us get you cleaned up and then I'll put some food into your belly."

Martyn nodded gratefully and followed him to a cab, waiting at Kings Cross, a hundred yards away.

***

When they arrived at Nilsen's apartment, he showed Martyn Duffey to the bathroom, gave the teenager a towel and a bar of soap and then inspected the floorboards for any strange smell before putting on a pot of pasta on the stove.

While the pasta was boiling, he went to the bathroom door and peeked through the keyhole.

He was in time to see Martyn take off his briefs and get into the bath. The boy's body was just about the youngest-looking Dennis had ever seen – even younger than Stevie – and it reminded him of Olav when he'd gone into Olav's bedroom and played with his penis all those years ago. Dennis clutched his crotch as Martyn turned around and revealed his firm little buttocks. *Tonight, your ass is mine, Martyn Duffy*, he thought, swallowing hard.

Ten minutes later, Martyn was scrubbed and dressed in one of Nilsen's t-shirts and a pair of shorts, sitting at the kitchen table.

Dennis was in front of the stove, adding coriander, rocket and chicken strips to the boiling fettuccini. He had taken off his work clothes and was now only wearing a vest and his boxers.

"How did you end up living at the railway station?" he asked quietly.

Duffey dropped his chin to his chest. "I'm a runaway. I used to be a catering student in Birkenhead but that decision was forced upon me by my parents. Catering is not what I want to do for the rest of my life, so I quit and took the train here four days ago." He stopped and wiped his wet hair from his forehead before continuing. "But I didn't have any money for the train fare and the Transport Police caught me out, so I was thrown off the train at Chester. From there I hitchhiked here and then spent three days at the station until you found me this afternoon."

"Bloody hell!" Nilsen exclaimed. "Where did you sleep?"

"On one of the benches behind Euston square," replied Martyn.

"That must have been tough and lonely."

"It was," Martyn Duffy said in a sombre tone. Then his voice grew urgent. "Sir, please don't call up my parents, please, please? They don't know where I am and I don't want to go back to Birkenhead."

Dennis pushed his eyeglasses up the bridge of his nose and smiled. "Your secret is safe with me, Martyn. I don't even know who your parents are or what their phone number is. Right now, my only responsibility as a civil servant is to make sure you're fed and that you have a roof over your head."

"You're a civil servant? What, like an officer of the law?"

"No, no. I work for Manpower Services. I help obtaining employment for people like you. That is why you are going stay here for the rest of the weekend and on Monday we're going to find you a job somewhere, okay?"

"Okay," said Martyn. "Thank you so much. You're like an angel."

The pasta was ready and Dennis Nilsen dished up in two large tin bowls before placing the fullest one in front of Martyn. Then he poured two glasses of milk and sat down across from the youth.

Martyn muttered a quick "Thank you" and then began to eat and drink greedily. Dennis could see that he was incredibly hungry and very much exhausted; his eyelids were drooping and the movement of his hands appeared sluggish.

"Do you like the food?" he asked.

"It's fantastic!" Martyn replied. "Where did you learn how to cook like this?"

"I was a chef in the army. Travelled all over the world while learning new recipes."

Mumbling something inaudible, Martyn Duffey returned his attention to the meal and they ate in silence after that.

When they had finished supper, Dennis stood up, gave Martyn a pat on the shoulder and then said, "Why don't you lie down on the bed? I can see that you are dead tired."

Martyn nodded his head slowly. "You're right. I'm out on my feet. Thank you for the food."

He approached the bed like a zombie and was asleep within a matter of minutes.

At first, Dennis wanted to go through with his plan of finding a job for Martyn Duffy after the weekend, but the more he looked at the sleeping teenager, the more his mind told him that this golden opportunity might not represent itself again in the near future.

Pacing around in the apartment for about half an hour, he finally picked up his necktie from where it was hanging over a chair and began to twist it into a ligature.

When the twisted tie was tight as a rope, he hurried over to the bed, wrapped the ligature around Martyn Duffy's neck in a flash and started strangling him with all his might. Duffy woke up and began to scream but, like Stephen Holmes, he only gurgled and rasped. He viciously kicked around with his legs and tried to insert his fingertips between the tie and his throat, but Dennis Nilsen was far too strong for the young man.

Nilsen held his grip until Martyn's limbs turned flaccid, as he fell into an unconscious state.

After this, Nilsen dragged the youth into his kitchen by his feet and left him on the floor while filling the basin with water. He was already aroused by the prospect of a second dead flatmate (*Three's company, Kenny*, he thought) and his erection was protruding like a periscope through the opening in his boxers.

When the basin was half-full, he pulled Martyn Duffy up by hooking his forearms underneath the boy's armpits from behind, then he pushed his head into the water and drowned the sixteen-year-old in the stainless steel basin like it was the easiest thing in the world.

Once Martyn was dead, Dennis undressed him and arranged him on his back on the kitchen floor before removing his own clothes.

Straddling the deceased body, he sat down on the upper legs, then enfolded his stiff penis with the teenager's limp one and began to rub vigorously. Like with his previous two victims, Dennis reached an orgasm within seconds and he once again ejaculated over the corpse, this time covering the stomach and ribcage in a pool of semen.

"You are so beautiful," he told the corpse. He bent down and kissed the fleshy lips, his tongue probing the inside of Martyn Duffey's lifeless mouth.

Dennis stood up and, upon attempting to pick up the cadaver, realized that his energy was drained. Instead, he grabbed hold of the feet and clumsily dragged the body to the bathroom. While the bath was running he went back to the kitchen to pour himself a rum and Coke with ice.

This time he got into the bath with the corpse and sat behind it as he sponged the semen from the torso with soap and lukewarm water, singing, *You are my sunshine, my only sunshine. You make me happy, when skies are grey*. Dennis really did feel he was in love with this one. He didn't know why but he just did. It was almost like the little birds he'd rescued and fed fish fingers to when he had been a young boy.

Following the bath and another masturbation session, he finished his rum and let Bleep back into the house.

Poor Martyn Duffey hadn't even met Bleep before his quick demise.

Then Dennis got into bed with his third corpse in seventeen months.

***

Duffey's dead body spent the next two days in the same cupboard that Kenneth Ockenden's corpse had occupied for eight hours and then, when it became too bloated, Dennis Nilsen stowed it beneath the floorboards, beside Ockenden's badly mutilated corpse.

A jab of guilt hit Nilsen in the chest just before he replaced the floorboards again.

Staring at Martyn Duffy's swollen face, he thought of the boy's parents back in Birkenhead. He hadn't seen anything on the news (he'd been in front of the telly a lot lately) but he was pretty sure they were worried sick about their teenage son.

Perhaps I should choose the older ones, like Ken, he thought. *At least the ones that are not minors anymore.*

The thought of his victims' families stayed with him for a long time and, after this third murder, Dennis Nilsen became increasingly disturbed. He began to think that he was a psychopath obsessed with having dead people around him, but he couldn't do anything about it. He understood that he was driven by his fears of loneliness and hoped that keeping bodies as mementos in his home would take this fear away, but his mind was not strong enough to process everything that had been going on.

CHAPTER 12

Following Martyn Duffey's murder, Nilsen's urge for more companions increased dramatically.

On the afternoon of August 20th, 1980 – an overcast but particularly hot day – he took the underground into London's West End to go watch a musical comedy show in Her Majesty's Theatre at Piccadilly Circus. The show was called *The Secret Policeman's Balls*, a production by John Cleese, featuring himself, as well as up-and-coming comedian, Rowen Atkinson, Scottish comedian, Billy Connolly, and music by Nilsen's favorite artist, Pete Townshend from the Who.

After the show, which was disappointingly short, he walked around and watched a bunch of street magicians, none of whom really excited him, before noticing a new vibrant pub just beyond the statue of William Shakespeare.

Dennis Nilsen crossed the street and went inside.

The place was modern with whitewashed walls and a slick granite bar counter. Behind the bar counter was a backdrop of sandblasted mirrors, advertising an assortment of beers and bourbons. There were about a dozen noisy patrons inside and, sounding from six state-of-the-art speakers, Robert Smith's voice was singing The Cure's popular hit single, *Boys don't cry*.

Sitting down at a rosewood table in the back, Dennis ordered a Guinness draught from a ginger waitress with slant green eyes, and then studied his surroundings.

Most of the people were in groups but there was one attractive man, somewhere in his late twenties, sitting alone at the bar, smoking a cigarette and drinking whiskey from a tumbler. He was wearing a tight-fitting pink t-shirt and his muscled arms were covered in tattoos. The man's jet-black hair and dark complexion reminded Dennis of Poncherello from his beloved television show.

He sipped on his Guinness while contemplating whether or not to approach the loner.

Halfway through the pint, he had gathered enough confidence and walked over to the bar with a Lucky Strike dangling from the corner of his mouth. Tapping the tattooed man on the shoulder, he said, "Excuse me, do you have a light for me?"

The man turned, revealing a clean-shaven face, and smiled. "Be my guest," he replied in a Scottish accent. He casually pushed a box of matches over the counter with two fingers.

Dennis thanked him and lit his cigarette before taking a seat.

"Will you watch my stuff for a second?" the man requested. "I need to take a pee."

"Sure," replied Dennis.

The "stuff" the guy was referring to comprised of a wallet, two packs of Marlboros and his matches on the bar counter. Once he was out of sight, Dennis opened the wallet and noticed a driver's license with credentials inside: *William David Sutherland, D.O.B: 05/05/1954.*

He did the calculation in his mind and thought, *Twenty-six. A full-grown man, like Ken Ockenden. That is much better than the two young ones*. The innocent adolescence of Stevie and Martyn was still gnawing at his nerves. It made him feel like a paedophile.

William Sutherland returned a minute later and sat down again. "Thank you," he said in a clear voice. "I'm Billy, by the way."

"Hello, Billy," replied Nilsen. "My name is Dennis. "You don't mind the company?"

"Not at all. Where are you from? You sound Scottish."

"Yup, Scottish all right. I'm originally from Aberdeenshire, but I've been living in London for almost ten years now. You?"

"Edinburgh," said Billy. He took a sip of whiskey and then added, "That's where I was born but I'm actually all over the place now. I guess you can call me a gypsy of some sorts."

Billy Sutherland was, in fact, a gypsy – as well as a male prostitute.

He didn't have a permanent address and never stayed in the same place for more than three or four weeks at a time. With no tertiary education or a formal occupation, he made his money by sleeping with desperate gay men all around Great Britain, or by pick-pocketing people at the underground railway stations.

Over the next hour, Billy made no secret of this irresponsible lifestyle and even attempted to solicit Dennis Nilsen for paid sex but Nilsen refused, telling Billy that he would never reimburse anybody for intercourse. However, the refusal did not cause any hostility between the two men. Dennis spoke about his days in the army and about his boring job at Manpower Services, while Billy returned with stories about his travels to Wales and Northern Ireland.

"You meet strange people in some of these places," said Billy Sutherland. "This one time I was in Cardiff and there was a Welshman who paid me fifty pounds to act dead while he masturbated over my body. Can you believe that?"

"Hmm, interesting," replied Dennis, dragging on his cigarette. A shiver ran down his spine and the hair stood up on the back of his neck.

Billy's eyes widened. "Interesting? No, no, no. That is not interesting, my friend. That is just plain fucked-up, if you ask me. I mean, really?" He finished his third tumbler of whiskey in a quick swig and beckoned the bartender for a refill.

Nilsen changed the subject. "So, what is the weather like in Wales?" The question wasn't just about making conversation; he'd never been to Wales and had always wondered what England's western neighbor's climate was like.

"Pretty much the same as here," replied Billy. "Only, they actually have real summers. Between June and August, you sometimes get as much as fifteen days of sunshine in a row."

"Bollocks!" exclaimed Dennis. Although he was used to Scotland's unpredictable summer days and London's miserable grey skies, he loved sunshine. He made a mental note to visit Cardiff during the following year's summer break.

"I shit you not," Billy assured him. "During the summertime in Wales, people are tanning on the bonnets of their bloody cars, man!"

A short while later, just before eight-thirty, the two men had finished their respective drinks and decided to visit some of the other establishments in and around Piccadilly Circus.

They continued to enjoy the evening and went pub-crawling until after eleven o'clock, when Dennis became tired and said, "Listen, Billy, it was great hanging out with you but I have to get into bed. Tomorrow is a workday for me, see?"

Billy gave him a sad look but accepted his new friend's "early" resignation from their night out.

Dennis made his way past the Shaftesbury Memorial Fountain and into the Leicester Square underground tube station, three hundred yards beyond that. When he fell into the queue to pay for his Northern Line ticket, he suddenly felt a pat on his back and turned around, startled.

To his surprize, Billy Sutherland was standing there, shrugging his shoulders.

"Look, Dennis, I have nowhere else to go," he said sheepishly. "Take me back to your place, please?" Then he dropped his voice to barely above a whisper and brushed up against Nilsen. "I am willing to sleep with you without expecting any payment. But I'm really broke after all the drinks. Will you at least pay for my tube ticket?"

**

Twenty minutes later, they were inside the apartment on Melrose Avenue, kissing furiously and tearing each other's clothes off. Bleep was not there to disturb them; it was still summer and she was sleeping in her little wooden shed, outside in the garden.

They got into bed and Dennis first performed oral sex on his visitor, until Billy reached an orgasm, before attempting to penetrate him anally.

Once again, like before, the problem was that his erection wasn't stiff enough to enter. At first, he thought he was too intoxicated, but then – when he stared at their naked bodies in the cupboard mirror – it struck him: Billy was moving too much; he was too… too *alive*.

"Lay still," Dennis told him firmly. "Otherwise this is not going to work."

"I can't," replied Billy. "I'm really sorry, but I have to take another pee. Just give me two minutes, okay?" He got up from the bed and walked to the bathroom.

Dennis gave a sigh. By now, he reckoned the size of Billy's bladder had to be smaller than Bleep's. It was about the tenth time that the man had to take a leak since they'd met four hours ago.

Climbing out of the bed slowly, Dennis Nilsen studied Billy, where he was standing in front of the toilet, urinating. He hadn't closed the bathroom door and he was swaying back and forth, making a terrible mess all around the toilet bowl and over the floor.

This guy is twice as drunk as I am, Nilsen grasped. *That cancels out his advantage of physical strength over me*. His train of thought was supported by the fact that while he had only been drinking beer the whole evening, Billy had been drinking much stronger whiskey, without any mix.

He bent down and silently removed his leather belt from his trousers on the floor. Then he made a lasso with the belt and slowly approached Billy from behind on tiptoes.

Billy Sutherland was just about to finish up when the loop of the leather belt slipped over his head and swiftly tightened around his neck. By the time he came to his senses and realized what was going on, the belt was cutting into the flesh of his throat so forcefully he could barely breathe. His muscles were flexing in panic and his heart was pounding with terror, while he felt the life drain from him like

England's melting snow in February. He was gasping for air so vigorously that his lips turned purple and his nose started bleeding.

Dennis kicked his heels against the toilet bowl, groaning, and then ripped the belt backward with brute force. In an instant, Billy Sutherland's neck snapped with a sharp crack and then he collapsed to the tiled floor, dead.

Nilsen glared at the naked body on the floor for a brief moment before crouching down to find that it had no pulse.

He was relieved beyond imagination.

A few minutes later, he was back on his bed with the corpse, thrusting his penis into its anal cavity while still pulling at the belt around the neck with both hands. He watched his movements closely in the mirror, panting, "Yes, my Billy-boy, that's how Des likes it. That's exactly how Des likes it." Streams of perspiration were running down the small of his back.

The gratification was so overwhelming that he achieved two orgasms in short succession.

Afterwards, he went through his usual ritual of bathing the cadaver, wrapping it in plastic bags and stowing it beneath the floorboards.

He now had a total of three corpses under his apartment.

It was getting crowded down there.

CHAPTER 13

By September 1980, it was time to make another plan once more.

Though Billy Sutherland's corpse was still fresh enough to exhume for television sessions, bathing and sexual entertainment, the badly decomposed bodies of Kenneth Ockenden and Martyn Duffey were eight months and four months old respectively.

These two rotting cadavers were now attracting insects and were infested with maggots and pupae. Whenever Dennis opened up the floorboards to take Billy out to watch television with him, he almost vomited upon noticing how the maggots and flies were crawling out of the ears, eye sockets and nostrils of the older corpses.

Flies were also present all around the apartment and the foul stench of decaying flesh filled the air. No matter how much insecticide he sprayed underneath the floorboards and in the lounge, the disgusting odor hung around. Dennis had lost all of his sexual appetite and the corpses were now a burden more than anything else. As a last resort, he used deodorants and perfume on the three dead bodies, to get rid of the smell and the flies and maggots, but nothing worked.

"This is becoming a clusterfuck," he told himself, staring down at the opening in the floorboards with his hands on his hips.

It was time for another bonfire, he realized, but a medium-sized fire in his backyard simply wouldn't suffice this time. He needed a big bonfire and more than just one rubber tyre in order to burn these three bodies and disguise the smell of burning flesh.

Staring through the back window of his lounge, Dennis noticed the waste ground beyond his garden and then it dawned on him: he would make a huge bonfire there. It was a cloudy autumn day and most of the trees had shed their leaves, but there was no breeze in the air. He knew he would be able to pull off a massive fire without the risk of burning down the entire neighborhood. The only issue was that the waste ground was visible from Park Avenue, so he could not exactly drag the bodies there, out into the open. Especially not at noon on a Saturday; too many looky-loos.

He had figured out a solution to this, but it was going to be an unpleasant one to implement.

After locking Bleep in the bathroom (telling her that he needed some privacy for a few hours) he walked to the kitchen, dragging his feet in procrastination of the next horrid task.

Returning to the opening in the floorboards with a number of refuse bags and an electric carving knife, Dennis Nilsen knelt down and laid some of the plastic bags down like a blanket. After he plugged the electric carving knife into a power socket against the wall, he dragged Kenneth's decomposed corpse up onto the bags and began to dismember its body parts with the serrated knife.

He first dissected the rotten head, then severed the floppy limbs and finally cut the torso full of maggots in half. He removed Kenneth Ockenden's shrunken, bloodless heart and set it aside on a clean dustbin liner. Then he placed all the other filthy body parts in another bag and laboriously repeated the procedure on the cadaver of Martyn Duffey, keeping the heart aside as well.

During these gruesome two hours, Dennis had to rush to the bathroom five times to throw up and he had a hard time keeping Bleep away from the mess in the lounge. Every time he opened the bathroom door, she ran toward the bodies and, after he'd been sick in the toilet or the basin, he had to catch her and lock her in again.

Billy Sutherland's body proved even more difficult to dismember than the other two, because very little decomposition had set in and the flesh was still tough, sticking to the hard skeleton like stubborn glue. Dennis went back to the kitchen to fetch a large meat cleaver. While chopping Billy's body up into pieces, it made him think of the butchering he'd done to the carcasses of cows and pigs while he had been a chef in the army. Billy Sutherland had not been dead for more than ten days. *About a week shy of well-matured beef,* Nilsen's twisted mind told him.

Once he had cut all three corpses into manageable pieces, he hauled the refuse bags with the human remains out into the backyard one by one. This was quite a strenuous undertaking; there were twelve bags in total, weighing four-hundred-and-eighty pounds collectively.

Outside, in the garden, he emptied the soil from three of David's garden tyres, then dragged them through the pedestrian gate and out onto the open space of the waste ground behind his apartment.

He then gathered dry leaves, twigs and wood from around the dump and started a fire, adding more and more wood until the car tyres would burn easily. He found two thick logs – which looked like telephone poles, only shorter – and arranged them on top of his bonfire. Once the pillar of flames was burning about twice as high as the fire he had scorched Stevie on, he walked around it and yanked the rubber tyres onto the logs in a triangle.

Now that he'd converted this blaze into the biggest bonfire he had ever seen, Dennis meticulously carried the bags with body parts from his garden and threw them on top of the burning tyres, two at a time, over a period of forty minutes. A few motorists slowed down but nobody stopped to ask him about the bonfire. They probably assumed he was burning junk and garden refuse, Dennis reckoned while looking around nervously.

When all the bags with body parts were engulfed in flames, he slumped down onto a pile of bricks in complete exhaustion.

He lit a cigarette and inhaled deeply as he watched the black smoke rise up from his communal bonfire and into the vanilla autumn sky of Cricklewood.

Emotionally, he felt like a free man for the first time in months.

His apartment was clean and he was ready for a fresh start.

CHAPTER 14

When his bonfire had burnt out, four hours later, it was dark outside and Dennis went back into the lounge to fetch the three hearts, still wrapped in a dustbin liner.

He poured himself a rum and fetched a spade from the broom cabinet before burying the hearts in the corner of his garden. When he had covered up the hole, he stepped onto the tiny organ-grave and said, "Cheers!" while holding up his glass. "Here's to Ken, Martyn and Billy. May your hearts forever be at peace, fellows."

This cleansing ritual caused Dennis Nilsen to go into another spiralling stupor.

For a period of sixteen days he didn't go to work (claiming that he had the measles) and drank himself into oblivion every single evening, mostly at home but occasionally at the *Cricklewood Arms* pub in Melrose Avenue. Voices in his head were beginning to tell him he was an evil murderer and that this condition would never be cured, not in a million years.

One morning, early in October 1980, he awoke next to the naked corpse of a pretty blond-haired man in his mid-twenties, without having any recollection of the previous night. He didn't know where he had met the man, how they had ended up in his bed, or how he had killed him. Nonetheless, the man wasn't breathing anymore and – based on his homicidal behavior over the past year, and on the demonic voices deep inside his head – Dennis knew for sure he was the executioner of yet another human being; his fifth.

Since he could not recall anything of relevance concerning this victim, he stowed Blondie's body under the floorboards as soon as he got out of bed, without simulating sex, masturbating, or wrapping it in plastic bags. In his distorted mind it was just another dead body and it meant absolutely nothing to him. In fact, the mere presence of this new corpse in his apartment repelled him.

What the event did achieve, however, was to caution Dennis to ease up on the drinking a little.

He had enjoyed his previous four killings because he was sober enough to remember the interaction he'd had with them before their deaths.

What is the point in killing someone if you cannot recall anything the next day? his subconscious asked him. *Where's the fun in that?*

***

A month later, in the first week of November, he went to the *Golden Lion* pub in Soho one evening but could not manage to start any meaningful conversations with any of the men inside.

Upon making his way back to the Leicester Square underground train station, he found a young English vagrant sleeping under a heap of newspapers in a doorway at the top of Charing Cross Road. The temperature in London had dropped to below forty degrees Fahrenheit. When Nilsen approached the man, he woke up and started muttering incoherent words. He was incredibly thin with a pale complexion and his entire body was shivering. He was also missing several teeth, Dennis noticed.

"Hey, what is your name?" he asked, feeling sorry for the homeless man.

The guy turned his back on him and grew silent.

"Look, I just want to help you," Dennis told him, crouching down. "It's bloody cold outside, man. Let me take you back to my place and give you something to eat and a bed to sleep in. Do you have any identification on you?"

Shaking his head, the man began to weep.

Dennis helped him up and hailed a taxi. He didn't want to risk taking the tube, in case they asked for ID at the ticket office.

During the taxi ride, the vagrant did not say another word but when they entered Dennis Nilsen's apartment, he mumbled, "Thank you very much for your kindness." He sat down on the floor in the lounge, playing with Bleep, while his host fixed him some food in the kitchen.

Nilsen gave his visitor bologna sausages, bread and two bottles of beer before tucking him into the bed an hour later. Then he poured himself a strong whiskey nightcap and settled in front of the telly. The feature film was Stanley Kubrick's *The Shining* and Jack Nicholson's wicked performance was so convincing that Dennis Nilsen couldn't help but thinking about murdering the man in his bed. This was not his initial plan, though. He really wanted to take care of the homeless man – whose name he still didn't know – and he somehow knew he was going to regret it if he killed this one.

Before the movie was finished, his empty whiskey glass was abandoned on the coffee table and Dennis was on top of his next victim's torso, strangling him with a necktie. The vagrant died fast and noiseless after his legs had moved around in a cycling motion for about three minutes.

Once the man's heart had stopped beating, remorse instantly washed over Dennis. He was livid with himself... and with the disturbing film that he believed caused him to go through with the act. Attempting to resuscitate his victim with mouth-to-mouth breathing, he began to sob uncontrollably. "I'm so sorry. I'm so sorry," he kept on saying to the corpse.

When he finally gave up on his reviving efforts, Dennis climbed off the bed and stood in front of the mirror. Spitting at his own image, he said, "Why did you do that, you sick bastard? Why? He was just a homeless man, damn it! That wasn't necessary, Des. Not at all."

After he had added the new cadaver beside the blond man's corpse underneath the floorboards, Dennis tried to comfort himself by reasoning that he had done the guy a favour.

His life as a nomad on the streets of London would have turned out one of long suffering anyway, he silently told himself.

***

His seventh victim was eighteen-year-old "blue-eyed Scotty" whom he'd met at the *Golden Lion* on January 4th, 1981. This murder was physically the most difficult one for Nilsen thus far, since he was so drunk he could barely manage to hold on to the necktie's ends as he strangled the young man in an armchair in his lounge.

It wasn't his fault, he felt afterwards. Yes, he had lured Scotty to his apartment, but it was Scotty who had initiated the drinking game called *I have never*.

They were sitting in front of the television, both still wearing work attire, when Scotty said, "Let's play 'I have never'. It's a drinking game." Bleep was on the carpet in the corner, cleaning her paws.

Dennis frowned. "I have never? How does that work?"

"It's quite easy," replied Scotty. "I start with something like 'I have never masturbated on a train'. Then you need to ask yourself whether you have ever done that. If the answer is 'no', I drink and it's your turn, but if the answer is 'yes' you have to down your drink and I get to go again."

"That sounds like fun," Dennis replied, chuckling. He retrieved a bottle of tequila and two shot glasses from the kitchen and poured two shots. Both of them were already fairly sloshed after happy hour at the pub, but they were going to pass out in the apartment anyway, so what the hell? Dennis Nilsen argued. "Off you go then," he told Scotty.

"I have never tried to suck my own you know what," Scotty slurred and then giggled.

"Damn you," said Dennis. He threw a shot of tequila down his throat and poured another one. "Next question," he told his guest.

Scotty scratched his chin and then said, "I have never slept with a woman."

Dennis downed another tequila.

"Really?" Scotty blinked his blue eyes. "I thought you said you were gay?"

"I am," replied Dennis. "It only happened once, when I was still in the army. It was an experiment of some sorts, but not a very pleasant one."

Scotty laughed. "Okay, here's the next one: I have never had sex in public."

Dennis shook his head and said, "Drink up, my friend. I'm afraid I haven't had the privilege."

After downing his tequila, Scotty smacked his lips and then shuddered. "All right, your turn again," he said, refilling his glass.

"I have never masturbated on a train," Dennis said, smiling. "Drink up, buddy."

"Bugger!" replied Scotty. "You caught me with my own example!" He drank a shot of tequila.

"I have never had a threesome," Dennis continued.

Scotty remained motionless and Dennis drank a shot. He was starting to feel lightheaded and the images around the lounge were blurry.

"I have never had sex with a guy in his sleep," Scotty slurred.

Nilsen drank.

"I have never had sex with a boy younger than eighteen."

Nilsen drank.

"I have never engaged in bondage games."

Whereupon Dennis Nilsen ripped off his tie and strangled Scotty to death.

It took longer than fifteen minutes. He was so inebriated that he lost his grip on the necktie several times and his strength was weakened to the point where he couldn't seem to get the deed done. Bleep was barking and jumping up and down in a panic. "What the hell are you doing to me?" Scotty kept on crying out in a rasping voice, kicking his legs against the base of the chair and shielding his face with his arms.

But, in the end, his defenses failed him and he finally stopped breathing when Dennis made a knot in the tie and managed to hold it tight for an extended period.

As Dennis let go of the necktie and slumped to the floor, Bleep began to lick his hands, as if he were the victim. "Oh, Bleep," he moaned, "why can't I stop this?" He rolled onto his back and thought about the words that initiated his fury: *bondage games*.

His mind wandered back to October 1979 and to a homosexual student from Hong Kong by the name of Andrew Ho.

He had met Andrew at a pub in St Martin's Lane and they had instantly liked each other. When Andrew Ho came to his apartment that evening, Dennis attempted to strangle him while Ho was performing oral sex on him. The student succeeded in wangling himself out of the strangulation and reported the incident to the police the following day. The police questioned Dennis that same day but then Andrew phoned them and told them that he was not going to press any formal charges – that it had just been innocent *bondage games*. After that, Dennis never heard from Andrew Ho again.

As his thoughts drifted back to the present, he patted Bleep on the back before dragging Scotty's lifeless body to the southern wall to bury him alongside Blondie and Nomad.

Prior to putting the floorboards back in position, Nilsen burst into tears while looking at his handiwork. On the television, the moving classical theme *Fanfare for the Common Man* announced the end of Channel 3's broadcast for the night and it only increased Dennis Nilsen's melancholy, causing him to cry even harder.

The next morning, he woke up on the half-rolled up carpet in the lounge, the three floorboards still standing against the wall. His head was throbbing and his mouth was dry as a dessert. The telly was still switched on and, as he came into an upright position, he noticed on the news a face he recognized. The banner at the bottom of the picture read: *Peter Sutcliffe, a.k.a The Yorkshire Ripper, had been arrested and charged with the brutal murder of thirteen women this morning.*

Nilsen's skin broke out in goosebumps. *That could have been me*, he thought, trembling.

CHAPTER 15

Sunday, March 29th, 1981 marked the very first London Marathon race, with over six thousand runners participating.

Dennis Nilsen went out to watch the spectacle that morning. It was a crisp spring day with clear blue skies and a slight breeze blowing in from a south-westerly direction. While this lazy Sunday started very well for Nilsen, it didn't end that well.

He took the tube to the Thames Embankment station and looked at the runners – aimlessly jogging alongside the riverbank – for about half an hour, after which he became bored and went to a pub for bangers and mash and a pint of Guinness. By noon, the pint had progressed to nine pints and he was "pissed out of his skull" he told the bartender. He picked up a gay Irishman from Belfast, whose name was too complicated to pronounce (it certainly wasn't something like Paddy McBride, Dennis later recalled) so he dubbed the young man "Belfast Boy".

They went to his apartment early in the afternoon and took a nap together to allow the alcohol to wear off. When Dennis awoke at dusk, Belfast Boy was dead beside him in his bed. Once again, as with Blondie, he had no idea how he had killed the Irishman, but the voices inside his head told him he had strangled the youngster with his bare hands. The pulsing pain in his wrists and thumbs confirmed this suspicion.

When he prised the floorboards open for the hundredth time, Dennis realized he had a conundrum to deal with: there was no more space for a fourth body.

"For fuck's sake," he muttered and then carried the corpse of Belfast Boy to the kitchen. He stowed it in the cabinet underneath the basin, gathered his electric carving knife and a roll of refuse bags and returned to the opening in the floorboards. Bleep was sniffing around, so Dennis let her out into the garden before resuming the grotesque task of dismembering the bodies once more.

Dragging out the decaying corpses one by one, he dissected them into smaller pieces and stashed these heads, arms, legs and sections of torsos in the plastic bags. He worked well into the night, taking four breaks – two to vomit and two to smoke cigarettes. By the time he was done, he packed the plastic bags with body parts beneath the floorboards and noticed that there was now space for Belfast Boy's body, but not in its current form. He would have to dismember the Irishman's corpse as well.

After all four bodies had been "packaged" and the floorboards were back in place, Dennis took a long bath and then let Bleep back in to keep him company.

All his other companions were gone; they had been butchered into pieces of meat.

He was alone again.

**

Exactly four months later, on Sunday, July 29th, Dennis was watching the royal wedding between Prince Charles and Lady Diana Spencer on television when there was a knock at the front door. Bleep was outside in the garden, so she didn't hear anything.

"Who's there?" he called without getting up. *Probably some Seventh-day Adventist*, he thought, *or a stupid vacuum cleaner sales rep.*

"It's your landlord, Mr Nilsen," came the answer.

Dennis Nilsen's blood ran cold. *Shit! What about the body parts?* Although the plastic bags were now keeping the maggots and flies in check, it was smack bang in the middle of summer and the sour stench of rotting flesh was beginning to surface once more.

"I'm coming," he called in a tiny voice.

He hurried to the bathroom to fetch a can of air freshener and sprayed the area around the southern wall of the lounge generously before opening the door.

"Good afternoon, sir," he greeted his landlord, a heavyset man in his fifties.

"Mr Nilsen," said the landlord, "may I come in?"

Dennis shook his head. "It's, uhm, it's a little untidy, sir. May I ask what this is about?"

"It's quite all right," the landlord replied, "I won't invade your privacy. The reason I am here is to inform you that we will be renovating these apartments in the near future, so I will be requiring you to vacate the property."

What? No, you cannot do this to me! Nilsen's lips were quivering when he said, "Uhm, but sir, this is… this is very unexpected. I don't have another place to live."

"I understand that, Mr Nilsen. That is why I am giving you two months' notice. You only have to vacate in the first week of October. That should give you ample time to look for another flat."

"But sir, I don't have the money to relocate. These furniture moving companies charge a fortune!"

"And we are more than willing to help, Mr Nilsen. The investors have agreed on a lump sum of one thousand Pounds for each tenant, in order to take care of any moving costs and to reimburse you for the inconvenience caused. In addition, we will let you keep the furniture that came with the apartment when you signed the lease agreement."

Dennis had nothing to say to that. It was an offer he couldn't afford to refuse. A thousand Pounds constituted a lot of money in 1981 and he estimated that the move (if he could find a place nearby) would cost him about four hundred Pounds. The remaining six hundred Pounds would be a nice buffer for any unforeseen expenses.

When he had seen the landlord off and closed the door behind him, his mind went into overdrive:

First, I have to get rid of this bloody foul odor. Then I need to find a new apartment. I will burn the remains on another bonfire the week before I move out; there will be less wind around by the end of September. Where the hell am I going to find time to do all of this crap? It's not like I'm doing nothing at work. Damn it!

He decided to skip the rest of the boring royal wedding and get to work right away.

Something Dennis had learned while he was an army chef was that the lean muscle meat wasn't the challenge when it came to preserving animal carcasses. It was the internal organs and intestines that caused the decaying smell. *The same has to apply to human bodies...* his mind told him. *Why haven't I thought about this earlier?*

Removing the floorboards once more, he took out all the packages and rummaged through them to gather the lungs, livers, kidneys, hearts, stomachs and intestines. There was very little blood left but the rotting odour was unbearable and it took some time to retrieve all the pieces. He had to use a kitchen knife to cut the organs from the torsos of some of the more recent corpses.

Over the next two hours, Dennis made five trips to Gladstone Park, not far from his apartment, every time filling a cooler box with organs and disposing of them in the bushes and shrubs of the quiet park. These organs would eventually be eaten by small animals such as squirrels and stray dogs, or just melt into the earth and become compost.

***

On September 17th, a week before Nilsen was planning to light his final bonfire, he walked out into a chilly Thursday morning on his way to work.

As he turned right onto the sidewalk, he noticed a man in his early twenties slumped against the wall separating the row of apartments from the street. The color was drained from his freckled face and he appeared to be in some pain.

Dennis rushed to the young man and said, "Good grief, are you all right?"

The guy groaned and replied, "It's my medication. It causes my legs to weaken." He took off his hat and exposed a pair of large ears and light brown hair in a crew cut.

"What's your name?" Dennis asked, pulling him up and supporting him with his right arm.

"I'm Malcolm Barlow," replied the young man.

"Will you be able to walk, Malcolm?"

"I can try."

Dennis assisted him up the pathway to the front door of 195 Melrose Avenue and quickly realized that something was very wrong with young Malcolm. His legs were barely able to support his body weight and his breathing was short and uneven. He was also burning up with a fever.

Once they were inside Nilsen's apartment, he made Malcolm comfortable on the sofa and then asked, "What kind of medication are you taking?"

"It's for my epilepsy," replied Malcolm. He retrieved a plastic container with pills from his jacket pocket and handed it to Dennis. "It inhibits the frequency of the epilepsy seizures but sometimes it affects my nervous system and then my legs become wobbly. It's never been this bad, though."

Nodding in comprehension, Dennis picked up the phone and called for an ambulance. He explained the situation to the 999 operator and when he read out the name of the medicine on the container, the operator told him that they'd had similar cases before and that an ambulance had been dispatched.

While they waited for the ambulance, Malcolm clarified that he was supposed to eat something before taking his medication but he had overslept and hadn't had time for breakfast. He also told Dennis that he was mentally handicapped and that he was receiving income support from England's Department of Health and Social Security.

The ambulance arrived in under ten minutes and once Malcolm Barlow had been taken to hospital Dennis went to work like any other weekday.

That evening, he phoned the hospital to inquire about Barlow and the nurse on duty told him the young man was in a stable condition and that he should be discharged the following day.

Upon returning from work on Friday, Dennis found Malcolm Barlow sitting on the stairs in front of his doorstep.

Malcolm smiled and rose to his feet. "See, I'm better now. I came by to say thank you."

Recalling what he had said the previous day about income assistance from the DHSS, Dennis asked, "Would you like to come in for dinner?"

"Sure, thanks," replied Malcolm.

Dennis prepared them boiled eggs with a selection of cold meat and cheeses before making the mistake of giving his young visitor alcohol. Malcolm had taken his medicine just an hour before and it took only two rum and Cokes for him to pass out on the sofa.

Staring at the sleeping man on the sofa, Dennis had one thought in his lonely mind: *What if he wakes up and leaves me to be on my own again?*

With the schedule 4 Lamictal medication now reacting to the alcohol, Malcolm Barlow was so out of it that he didn't even wake up when Dennis chocked the life out of him with his bare hands, twenty minutes after he had fallen asleep. In stark comparison to Blue-eyed Scotty, this was by far the easiest of the nine cold-blooded murders Dennis Nilsen had committed while living on Melrose Avenue.

Once Barlow was dead, Nilsen stored his body beneath the basin in the kitchen and then switched on the television to learn that a Russian Aeroflot passenger airplane with 33 people on board had been struck by a Soviet Army helicopter on a training mission earlier that day. All 33 plane passengers – and 7 on the helicopter – had been killed.

Sipping his rum, Dennis wondered what 40 dead people would look like when piled up in a heap.

He was mesmerized by the thought of lifeless people. During the past three years of his life, he had figured that much out. His interaction with corpses had been much more meaningful than the contact with human beings walking around, breathing and talking. He clearly understood that this was unconventional behavior but he just couldn't stop himself. Dead bodies aroused him, intrigued him and fascinated him.

He couldn't get enough of the deceased.

CHAPTER 16

The final bonfire at 195 Melrose Avenue was a monster.

In addition to wood, grass and leaves found around the waste ground behind his garden (as well as three more car tyres) Dennis also added four cupboard doors to this fire.

His landlord had paid him a visit the previous day and showed him a nice place on Cranley Gardens Street in the Muswell Hill district of North London. This flat was much smaller than the apartment on Melrose Avenue, but he didn't need such a big place anyway, so he signed a one-year lease agreement. The new flat also had built-in wardrobes and there was only enough space for one of the three cupboards Dennis Nilsen owned. He had unscrewed the door hinges of the two older cupboards and was now adding these doors to his big bonfire.

It was 6:35 a.m. on a cool and misty morning, the last Saturday in September 1981.

Once the doors were in place – effectively creating four walls around the fire – he drenched the base of twigs and leaves in mineral turpentine and set it alight. Then he went back into his apartment and began to transfer the refuse bags with body parts from beneath the floorboards to the large bonfire. In-between carrying the bags to the fire, he also burned some other items he wouldn't need at his new place: a dusty old carpet, Dee-Dee's wooden cat house, a pile of obsolete work documents, a broken clock and two dilapidated bed lamps.

At one stage during the morning, three kids crossed Park Avenue and started dancing and playing around the fire. Dennis reckoned if he chased them away they would tell their parents, so he left them alone and carried on with his business as if it was nothing more than a house cleaning exercise.

"What'cha burnin' Mista?" the one boy asked, standing with his hands on his hips and cocking his head to the side. Dennis estimated him to be about seven or eight years old.

"Oh, just some old rubbish," he replied casually. "I'm moving out next week and I need to get rid of all the stuff I won't be using in my new house."

The answer seemed to satisfy the kids and they continued their dancing and skipping around his mass funeral pyre. It was giving off a tremendous heat, Dennis suddenly realized.

"Don't come too close to the fire, now, you hear?" he warned them.

They retreated a bit and the leader from earlier replied, "You got it, Mista."

With layers and layers of wood varnish on them, the cupboard doors burned like the fires from hell and the human remains and other flammable items were incinerated as soon as they made contact with the licking flames.

After all the bags with pieces of Blondie, Nomad, Scotty and Belfast Boy had been added to the bonfire, Dennis went back to Bleep's shed in the garden to retrieve Malcolm Barlow's corpse. He had stashed it in the shed when his landlord had knocked on the apartment's door the previous day.

Dennis now dragged this cadaver back into the lounge, onto a layer of dustbin liners, and got to work with his carving knife, dismembering Malcolm's body. During all of this, Bleep was locked in the bathroom with enough food and water and her favorite blanket to sleep on.

By the time Malcolm's remains had been added to the bonfire, the sun was high up in the sky and the mist had disappeared together with the playing kids. Dennis went into the bathroom and picked Bleep up. Holding her close to his chest, he walked to the back window in the lounge and looked outside.

"What do you think of my bonfire, Bleep?" he said. "It's pretty, isn't it?" He then fetched a beer from his fridge, lit a cigarette and watched the fire burn through the window for the rest of the afternoon. In those moments, Dennis thought of it as his *bonfire of vanities* (not knowing that six years later the novelist, Tom Wolfe, would write a book with the same title).

At 6:45 p.m. Dennis Nilsen went out into the twilight and inspected the residue of the fire. Between the warm ashes, cinders and cremated debris, he noticed a few large bone splinters and two intact skulls, which he crushed into smaller fragments with a shovel. Bleep was keeping her distance, remaining twelve feet behind her master, watching him work.

Satisfied that most of the evidence had been destroyed, Nilsen went back to his apartment where he replaced the floorboards in the lounge and nailed them shut. He fed Bleep while running a hot bath and climbed into the bathtub shortly after eight o'clock that evening.

As with the previous two bonfires, the day's activities felt like a cleansing process to Nilsen and he started crying hard while he lay in the steaming bath. He couldn't understand why he kept on killing people all the time. He had absolutely no control over it. It just kept on happening, as if it was happening to someone else.

"Why, Des?" he asked himself, sobbing. "Why do you keep on doing this? Why can't you just live your life like a normal person?"

Wiping tears from his cheeks with the back of his hands, he decided to make a fresh start at Cranley Gardens. *No more murders, okay?* his confused mind told him. *No more murders and no more of this obsession with dead bodies. You are done after today, Des Nilsen. Done.*

CHAPTER 17

Cranley Gardens Street was situated in the quiet neighborhood of Muswell Hill, a middle class part of North London. It was lined with tall three-story, semi-detached houses, built mostly with face brick façades in an Old English style.

The house at number 23 Cranley Gardens had been converted into three smaller flats and Dennis Nilsen's rental place was on the top storey; the attic flat. The first entrance door was on the ground level, on the left hand side of the building, and a flight of carpeted stairs led to a second door on the third floor, opening onto the flat itself.

On the inside there was a short hallway, serving as a makeshift kitchen to Nilsen, with a tiny bathroom beyond that. To the right was the lounge – which he had furnished with the sofa and two armchairs from Melrose Avenue, as well as a new tea chest in one corner – and past that was a small bedroom which was much warmer than the rest of the flat, courtesy of a fancy electric fireplace.

Dennis had lived there for almost two months when he woke up one Monday morning and decided not to go to work. It was November 23rd 1981, a crisp winter day in London, and he was celebrating his thirty-sixth birthday. After making himself a breakfast of scrambled eggs and leftover lamb shank, he took Bleep for a three-hour stroll in Hyde Park before returning her to the flat and making his way to his favorite gay-friendly pub, the *Golden Lion*, for lunch.

Sipping on a pint of Guinness, Dennis was silently praising himself for not attempting to strangle anybody to death since he'd moved out of the apartment on Melrose Avenue, when an incredibly handsome young man sat down next to him at the bar counter. He was lean and tall with dark black hair and a contagious smile. Judged by the way he was staring at the other men in the pub, Dennis instantly knew he was gay.

"What can I get you to drink?" the bartender asked the newcomer.

"You look like a nice enough bloke to me," said Dennis before the young man could answer. "Allow me to buy you a drink. I'm Des Nilsen, the *Golden Lion's* most loyal local customer."

"Paul Nobbs, nice to meet you, Des," the newcomer replied in a friendly tone. "And thanks for the offer. I'm a student so I won't say no to a free drink. No, sir."

"What will it be then?" inquired the bartender, slightly irritated.

Paul Nobbs glanced at Nilsen's Guinness. "I'll have what he's having."

"Where do you study?" Dennis Nilsen asked him. "I haven't seen you around here."

"At the University of London, up the road," Nobbs answered, "but I usually go to the *Champion* pub in Bayswater for drinks."

His pint arrived and he took a long sip.

Dennis lit a Lucky Strike with a disposable lighter. "What do you study?"

"It's a three year course called Eastern European studies. I'm in my first year now." Paul also lit a cigarette and then asked, "What do you do for a living?"

"I used to be a policeman but now I am working for Manpower Services. That, however, is not important." Dennis raised his glass. "What *is* important is that you came here as if being sent, Paul. It is my birthday today and I have nobody to celebrate it with." He winked in the direction of the bartender. "Except for Grumpy over there."

Paul laughed and also raised his glass. "Well, here's to you then, Des. Happy birthday!"

The words were like music to Dennis Nilsen's ears. This was the first time since Grandpa had died that someone sincerely wished him a happy birthday. Sure, his work colleagues congratulated him every year but that was more out of politeness than anything else, he knew.

He bought Paul Nobbs another two rounds of beer and then they went shopping at *Foyles* bookshop, not too far from the *Golden Lion*. Paul had expressed his love for literature earlier and he wanted to buy Nilsen a book for his birthday, regardless of his desperate financial position. "I would have spent the money on the beer you bought me anyway," he argued. Books were still very affordable back in 1981 and the prices at *Foyles* were cheaper than anywhere else in London.

By the time they came out of the bookshop, with a paperback copy of Sidney Sheldon's *Rage of Angels* tucked under Nilsen's arm, the sun was going down and it was bitterly cold outside. He invited Paul for a hot meal at his flat and they took the underground tube to Highgate station. From there they completed the fifteen-minute walk up Muswell Hill Road, both of them hugging their coats against the freezing wind, until they turned into Cranley Gardens Street and reached Dennis Nilsen's humble abode at number 23.

Dennis introduced Paul to Bleep and then he baked pork chops and made mashed potatoes for supper. Paul helped where he could but he wasn't very handy in the kitchen.

After they had eaten, they watched television, fondled each other and drank rum until after midnight. With his lean and fit body, Paul Nobbs got wasted in no time. His system simply wasn't used to drinking hard liquor at the same pace as his host.

"Let us get some sleep," Dennis suggested when he noticed the time. "You won't find a taxi now, it's past midnight already."

Paul agreed and they got into bed together. He fell asleep long before Dennis Nilsen, since he was already out on his feet from all the rum.

Staring at Paul's face while stroking his hair, the voices inside Nilsen's head began to ring in his ears once more: *What if he leaves you in the morning? Then you will never see this beautiful man again.* The moonlight was shining through the skylight window, casting a brilliant glow over Paul's relaxing face. His chest heaved rhythmically up and down with even breaths.

Dennis tried to resist but before he could help himself, he had one of his ties around Paul's neck and was strangling him out of consciousness. Paul Nobbs was so inebriated that he didn't even wake up properly from his stupor. His eyes flashed open for a second, then he made a soft moaning sound and lost consciousness. Dennis slowly pulled the tie back and dropped it on the floor beside the bed.

Before he could climb out of bed to fill a bucket of water to drown the unconscious young man in, sanity returned and he whispered to himself, "No, you're not going to kill him, Des. You're in a new place now, do not mess this up. Stay clean this time, please?"

Miraculously, it worked.

He leaned over to the bedside table to retrieve a glass of water he'd left there the previous evening and then poured it over Paul's face.

Paul Nobbs crashed back to consciousness with a loud yelp. Then his breathing returned to normal and he turned on his side to sleep off the alcohol in his system. At the foot of the bed, Bleep was snoring like a buzz saw. Dennis gave a sigh of relief and lay awake for another half hour before drifting into a restless sleep.

The next morning, Paul was up and about before him. When Dennis sat upright, the man was standing in front of a mirror on one of the built-in closets, studying his own image. Bleep was sniffing around at his feet.

He noticed Nilsen was awake and turned around. "What happened to me?" he asked in a hoarse voice. "I can't remember anything about last night. At least not since after we've had supper."

"You look bloody awful!" Dennis Nilsen exclaimed. "You should see a doctor."

That much was true. Paul's face was swollen, his eyes were bloodshot and he sounded like a croaking bullfrog. Dennis instantly regretted what he had done the previous night. But Paul Nobbs was alive and that in itself was a moral victory for what Dennis had now labelled a "recovering serial murderer". He knew in his heart that this was a colossal paradox, but that was the only term his chaotic mind had mustered ever since he moved into his new flat.

"I need to go now," Paul said absently, while gathering his clothes from the floor and getting dressed in a hurry.

"Don't you want coffee?" asked Dennis.

"No," replied Paul. "I really need to go." He looked at his wristwatch, struggling to focus his vision. "My classes start in less than an hour."

After Dennis had seen his visitor out with a polite, "Thank you for a lovely evening," he eased the door shut and told his dog: "See, everything is going to be okay, Bleep. We can live a normal life. Everything is going to be okay."

Unfortunately for Dennis Nilsen, that was as far from the truth as what the next eighteen months of his life would reveal.

CHAPTER 18

He met his next victim, twenty-three-year-old John Howlett, in March 1982 while drinking in the *Coleherne*, an infamous homosexual hangout located close to Leicester Square.

During those early months in 1982, Dennis Nilsen mostly kept to himself during daytime and spent nearly every night in a pub. He only had three goals in life by then: getting a promotion at work, finding a boyfriend, and caring for Bleep as best as he could. He had been promised a promotion in June and his companionship with his dog was growing stronger, but a long-term romantic relationship with someone else still eluded him.

After he had lured John Howlett from the *Coleherne* to his flat in Cranley Gardens, Nilsen poured them whiskeys (he was fresh out of rum for the first time since he'd moved in) and they settled in front of the television. The film was *For your eyes only*, with the charismatic actor Roger Moore playing James Bond in this instalment.

"I liked Sean Connery more," Howlett commented after the opening scene.

This declaration amused Dennis somewhat, because John's personality had a remarkable resemblance to Roger Moore.

"I disagree," he said. "He was too stiff to be a proper James Bond. Roger is confident but relaxed and that's how I think 007's character comes out best."

John Howlett sipped on his whiskey and then scratched his chin. "Do you remember that flash in the pan? The guy who only played Bond once in *Her Majesty's Secret Service*?"

"Oh, yes," Dennis replied. "He was absolutely useless. What was his name again?"

"George Lazenby."

Dennis nodded. "Yup. George bloody Lazenby. Great guy, but a useless James Bond if you ask me. No wonder they brought Connery back after that."

"Listen, Dennis," said Howlett, "I'm not feeling too well. Do you mind if I lie down in the room for an hour or so?"

Waving a dismissive hand, Dennis replied, "Be my guest. I'll wake you in an hour." Though, in his mind, he was livid. How could John just leave him to watch the movie by himself? He loathed watching television without company. Yes, Bleep was sitting by his feet but that wasn't enough. He was just beginning to enjoy the James Bond conversation with Johnny and now he had gone to bed.

As he drank faster and faster, Dennis Nilsen was working himself up to a crescendo over the sudden loss of camaraderie. He knew he had to take it slow on the booze because it usually caused the aggressive Dennis to surface, but he just couldn't stop himself.

He had an overwhelming urge to take Johnny's life.

Halfway through the movie, his fingers were digging so hard into the armchair's cushion that his knuckles turned white. Then he felt it: an upholstery strap under the cushion. He ripped the strap off and rushed to the bedroom.

Once he had the upholstery strap firmly around John Howlett's neck, a ferocious struggle followed. The more Dennis strangulated Johnny, the stronger he seemed to become. He was kicking and growling and he had his hands around his attacker's throat so firmly that Dennis believed *he* was going to be the victim instead of the killer in this murder. When he finally got the upper hand and John's fingers let go of his throat and the body became limp under Dennis Nilsen's weight, he shouted, "Holy shit!" His hands were shaking and his throat was burning like a bonfire. He couldn't believe how nearly the guy had overpowered him. John Howlett had fought back even harder than Blue-eyed Scotty had done back in Melrose Avenue.

Suddenly, Howlett began to stir again and Dennis smashed the upholstery strap so hard into his neck that his skull struck the headrest of the bed and blood started flowing out of a large gash in the back of his head. Then he stopped breathing for a second time.

Dennis fell onto Howlett in exhaustion and realized the man's heart was still beating.

Not letting go of his grip on the strap around John Howlett's neck with his right hand, he dragged him to the bathroom and clumsily opened both bath taps with his left. Blood was dripping everywhere and it made Dennis nauseous; he hated blood.

He quickly put the plug in the bathtub and pushed John's head down as far as he could. His victim wasn't struggling anymore but he didn't want to take any chances. The event had been stressful enough up to now. Bleep came running into the bathroom and Dennis chased her out just as the water level rose up to John's shoulders, his upside-down head now completely submerged in the crimson pool of water in the tub.

Johnny Howlett drowned four minutes later.

Leaving the dead body in the bathtub, Dennis rose to his feet and looked at himself in the mirror. There were red finger marks around his neck and scratch marks beneath his eyes and on his temples. "What the fuck have you done, Des?" he asked his image in the mirror. "You almost got yourself killed, you dumb bastard! And what about your promise to not murder anybody again, huh? What about that, you sick son of a bitch?" He couldn't recall when last he had been so disgusted with himself. Apparently still unable to quell his homicidal impulses, he now knew he had been wrong in being so relaxed after the Paul Nobbs incident.

When Dennis shifted his gaze back to the fresh corpse in the tub, something disturbingly problematic struck him...

Here at the attic flat on Cranley Gardens, he had no convenient floorboards, and no access to a garden.

How the hell am I going to get rid of the body? he thought in horror.

***

Howlett's cadaver stayed in the bath for three days, fully dressed in a pair of jeans, a sweatshirt and a bomber jacket.

During this time, Dennis Nilsen went to work as usual but he was a troubled man. He couldn't for the life of him figure out what to do with the dead body. In the evenings, he would glare at the bloated corpse in the bathtub while washing his hands, armpits and face in the basin.

When the weekend arrived, he finally composed himself and found a way to dispose of the corpse. On Friday evening, he stripped naked and got to work.

After removing the clothes from John Howlett's body, Dennis used a large carving knife to sever the head. There was a big pasta pot in the kitchen, which he filled halfway with water and then began to boil the head on his gas stove.

While the head was boiling, he went back to the bathroom to split the torso open from neck to navel with the carving knife and then he removed the internal organs. Making use of a sharp chopping knife, he sliced all these organs and intestines into smaller portions of meat on a wooden chopping board. He rolled the pieces into balls the size of peaches, covered them in toilet paper and flushed them down the lavatory one by one. This was a tedious process and it took more than three hours. By eleven o'clock that night, Dennis had flushed the toilet eighty-five times and he was lightheaded and weary.

He took a short break, smoked two cigarettes, and then used a serrated bread knife to saw off the hands and feet of the corpse. After slicing as much of the meat from the bones as was possible with the chopping knife, he crushed the phalanges and flushed the pieces of flesh and fragmented bones down the lavatory as well. Dennis repeated this procedure with the forearms and upper arms, working well into the small hours of the morning.

When he went to bed after three o'clock, the head was still boiling on the stove and the mutilated cadaver in the bathtub consisted of a torso and two legs only.

The next morning Dennis Nielsen got up at 9:00 a.m. and walked to a hardware store down the street where he bought four pounds of lime powder and a roll of heavy-duty plastic refuse bags. Upon returning to his home, he dismembered the legs and placed them in a refuse bag together with the torso before pouring lime powder inside and sealing the bag.

All that remained of the broiled head in the pot was a skull, which he placed in another refuse bag. The two bags were stowed in one of the unused wardrobes in his room and the meaty liquid in the pasta pot was washed down the drain.

After cleaning the tub and the bathroom floor with bleach, Dennis took Bleep for a walk and a wave of relief flooded over him. He had dotted the i's and crossed the t's, he believed. He was in the clear again, although he didn't know how long it was going to last.

He was addicted to killing human beings and there was no way of predicting who the next victim was going to be…

CHAPTER 19

Carl Stottor regarded himself as one of the friendliest men in London.

He was twenty-one years old with long blond hair and soft facial features. His theatrical personality was perfect for his job as a revue artist and, with a stage name of Khara le Fox, he wasn't shy about his homosexuality at all.

On a mild evening in May 1982, Carl met Dennis Nilsen in the *Black Cap* pub in Camden High Street. He didn't particularly like the *Black Cap*, but his boyfriend had ditched him the previous day and he knew that all the hotties were usually hanging out in and around Camden High. Tonight, Carl Stottor was wearing a flamboyant silver suit over a purple silk shirt.

"Why do you look so depressed?" Dennis asked him an hour or so after they had been introduced. "You're just about the sexiest man I have ever met and it's really sad to see you with that worried look in your eyes."

"My boyfriend dumped me yesterday," replied Carl, his bottom lip trembling.

Dennis tightened his jaw. "I'm sorry to hear about that. Were you close?"

"Very close. He used to attend all my drag queen performances, always bringing along a bunch of flowers, and then he just suddenly stopped about a week ago. When I confronted him about it yesterday, he broke out in tears and told me there was someone else and that he didn't love me anymore. That totally blew my mind and my heart was so shattered I couldn't sleep last night. I finally took two sleeping pills and crashed at four o'clock this morning. Now, everything is dull inside and I'm trying to process the miserable fact that I'm single after all these years."

"Well, Carl," said Dennis, stirring the ice in his rum around with two fingers, "if it will make you feel any better: I've been single all my life."

"Really? You've been gay your whole life and you've never had a boyfriend, like ever?"

Shrugging his shoulders, Dennis sighed. "What can I say? I guess I'm the unluckiest guy in the whole of England. The only companion I've ever had is Bleep."

Carl frowned. "Bleep?"

"My Collie dog. We're the best of mates. Have always been, will always be."

"I'd love to meet Bleep," Carl said in a high-pitched voice. "It's such an adorable name."

***

A little over forty minutes later they were in Dennis Nilsen's lounge, Carl drinking a stiff whiskey on the rocks and Dennis nursing a rum and Coke. Bleep was curled up on the carpet, watching television with them. Although the windows were open, a strange aroma was creeping up Carl Stottor's nose. He didn't mention anything to his new friend, but in the back of his mind was the thought: *It smells like old lamb stew, mixed with bleach or oven cleaner.*

They drank and chatted until shortly after ten, whereupon Carl couldn't keep his eyes open anymore. He only had three hours of sleep the previous day. When Dennis suggested they go to bed together, Carl replied, "No, please. I don't know if I'm ready for another relationship just yet. Would you mind if I rather slept on the sofa?"

"Not at all," said Dennis. He fetched a sleeping bag from his bedroom and laid it out on the sofa in the lounge. "Bleep will watch over you," he told Carl, "and please mind the zipper on the sleeping bag. It's kind of broken and quite tricky to open once it's zipped shut."

He didn't know at the time that this statement would later be used against him in a court of law, proving that it showed he had intent to murder Stottor.

Carl Stottor dozed off in the sleeping bag, wearing only his pink underpants, and awoke in terror later that night. He was suffocating, as the sleeping bag was strangling him, the zipper biting into his throat. Carl believed Dennis was trying to help him when he briefly heard him whisper, "Stay still, Carl," before everything went black around him. He fell unconscious.

When he awoke the second time, he was in a bathtub filled with cold water. He could hear water running and his vision was blurred. Carl was about to take a deep breath before a hand pushed his head beneath the water. He lurched upward in a panic and managed to free his head from the grip but then the hand pressed down again. For a second time, Carl freed his head from the grasp. He inhaled sharply and screamed, "No more, please! No more!" The hand pressed down again as he was about to take another breath and then everything went black once again.

His next memory was of Bleep licking his face and someone's hands massaging his chest. When his eyes fluttered open, broad daylight was shining through the windows where he sat in an armchair in Dennis Nilsen's lounge. He was dressed in an unfamiliar red tracksuit with a brown blanket over his knees. Dennis was crouched over him.

"What happened?" Carl mumbled, shaking his head in perplexity.

"Oh, Carl!" Dennis cried out. "You had a nightmare and then you got tangled up in the sleeping bag and nearly suffocated to death!"

Carl's hands went to his throat. "Yes, I remember that. But... but why did you try to drown me?"

Dennis threw his arms in the air. "No, no! You were in shock and I was trying to revive your blood circulation. That's why I put you in the cold water. Then you lost consciousness again and I dressed you and rubbed your limbs and heart to bring you back to life." Dennis made a sad face and embraced Carl. "I'm so glad you're alive," he said quietly. "I was worried sick about you, man."

Over the following two days, Dennis stayed at home (family responsibility leave, he'd told his office) and helped Carl to regain his strength. By the end of day two, Carl Stottor a.k.a Khara le Fox could breathe and walk properly again and Dennis saw him off with the words: "I hope we meet again…"

He was desperately trying to put a stop to his killing-spree.

So far, so good, he thought to himself. *I have saved two and killed only one. Paul Nobbs and Carl Stottor were lucky. Johnny Howlett pulled the short straw, but that was his own fault. He abandoned me for no other reason than "not feeling too well".*

***

Dennis Nilsen wasn't in a happy space at Cranley Gardens.

On many nights – upon returning home after unsuccessful attempts to solicit vulnerable young men – he would masturbate in bed, fantasizing about the ones he had cremated on his three bonfires at Melrose Avenue: Stephen Holmes, the cute young Irish lad, Ken Ockenden, the Canadian traveller and Martyn Duffy, the youth with the tight buttocks. Then there was Billy Sutherland, the butch fellow with the tattoos, Nomad of downtown London, Blondie, Blue-eyed Scotty, Belfast Boy and Malcolm Barlow with his epilepsy and his income from the Department of Health and Social Security.

Nine victims in total.

Nine images of naked corpses printed into Nilsen's mind so vividly that he reached an orgasm on demand whenever he recalled their earlobes, their eyes, their smooth skin and their soft genitals. Melrose Avenue had been a happy place, whereas Cranley Gardens was a butcher shop. He still flinched when he thought of the night when he'd boiled Johnny Howlett's head and hacked his body to pieces before flushing everything down the drain like medical waste.

Howlett's torso and legs were still in the black refuse bags inside the wardrobe and Dennis added lime powder every second week to keep it from decaying too fast.

No, his attic flat on Cranley Gardens Street didn't bring him any joy.

He did, however, receive some good news in June 1982. He was officially promoted to the position of Executive Officer – with additional supervisory responsibilities – at Manpower Services. With this promotion, he was also transferred from Denmark Street to another Job Center in Kentish Town, which was farther away from his flat, but that didn't bother Dennis too much. The idea of exploring a different part of London excited him.

CHAPTER 20

Graham Archibald Allen stumbled down Shaftesbury Avenue, Soho, in the early autumn breeze of September 1982, thinking about the last five years of his life with muddled memories.

Originally from Motherwell, he was a twenty-seven-year-old drunk and a junkie who had been in and out of prison and rehabilitation centers for most of his adult life. His relationship with his girlfriend and his son was down the drain and his life in London was one big haze of drug-infused, delinquent events. The last words he had heard from his girlfriend before he had left her family house earlier that evening was, "Fuck off and never come back!"

After that, he had walked to Piccadilly where he scored some crack and a few Pounds from a girl who owed him a favour. Then Graham Allen had sat in a pub for three hours, drinking beer with whiskey chasers, until he was out of cash. Now he had to walk (stagger) home, at the dreaded hour of midnight, because he couldn't afford a train ticket.

Studying all the taxis in Shaftesbury Avenue through his foggy vision, he wondered whether one of them would give him a free ride. No harm in asking, right?

As he approached one of the taxis, a man in a dark grey suit rushed across the street and took his arm. "Sir," he said, "are you all right? You look drowsy."

"I'm drunk and I'm high," Graham slurred. "Leave me alone."

"What's your name?" asked the man, peering over the rim of his glasses.

"Graham."

"Look, Graham, I'm Dennis and, if you want to, you can come back to my place for drinks, something to eat and a warm bed. What do you say? I'll even pay for your taxi ride."

Graham Allen thought he had just hit the jackpot. The drugs from earlier were wearing off and he could sure as hell do with a few more drinks. A free meal would be the cherry on the cake – he hadn't eaten since that afternoon and it was now 11:45 p.m. He grimaced. This was too easy, there had to be a trick to the guy's offer.

"Thank you," he said, staring at Dennis Nilsen with wide eyes. "But why on earth would you do that? You don't know me from a bar of soap."

"I work for Manpower Services," Nilsen replied, the corners of his mouth twitching. "It's my job to look after homeless people."

"I'm not homeless…" Graham Allen started saying, but then his words trailed off. Considering what his girlfriend had told him earlier, this statement was technically not true. He was sort of homeless at that moment.

***

When Dennis opened the kitchen cupboards in Cranley Gardens twenty minutes later, he realized he had very little provisions left for the month. There was a large tray of eggs, however.

"Listen, Graham," he said, peering at the drunk where he was sitting at the kitchen table. "I know it's past midnight already but can I make you an omelette? I don't have a lot of ingredients…" He opened the refrigerator door and then added, "I can do olives, cheese and mushrooms."

Graham Allen nodded his head. "Anything, my friend. I'm starving."

Bleep was asleep in the bedroom and Dennis decided not to wake her and introduce Graham to her. Whipping up a four-egg omelette in no time, he ceremoniously placed the plate in front of his guest. "Bon appétit," he said, smiling.

"Thank you so much," Graham managed before starting to devour the meal.

Halfway through his omelette, though, something very peculiar happened to Graham Allen. He fell asleep sitting upright on the kitchen chair.

Nilsen stared at the strange sight.

The man's head had awkwardly fallen to the one side, a piece of omelette still in his mouth, and he was snoring loudly through his nose. If it wasn't for the snoring, Dennis Nilsen would have thought him to be dead already.

Still amazed by how quickly Graham had fallen asleep – *While sitting up straight!* Dennis thought incredulously – he casually poured himself a nightcap, then removed his necktie and strangled Graham Allen to death in under three minutes. He couldn't believe how easy it was to drain the life from the intoxicated man.

The voices inside his head began to speak to Dennis again:

He didn't even put up a struggle, the useless bastard.

What an excuse for a human being.

Oxygen thief...

Once Allen's heart had stopped beating, Dennis released the tie ligature from the neck and undressed the dead body. He placed the naked corpse on its back on the floor and proceeded to masturbate with one hand while rubbing the limp penis of the deceased man with his other hand. When he was done, he dragged the cadaver to the bathroom where he washed it and left it in the bathtub.

The same as with Johnny Howlett, Dennis waited three days – until the weekend – before he dismembered Graham Allen's corpse.

After getting in the nude, he removed the body from the bath on Friday night. Laying two refuse bags on the bathroom floor, Dennis carefully positioned the body on it and then systematically began the task of dissecting it in the same manner as the previous cadaver.

He first cut off the head and once again boiled it in the large cooking pot on his stove. Then he severed the hands and the feet, diced the flesh and flushed it down the lavatory. He followed the same procedure as he'd done to Howlett with the internal organs. Next, he severed the body at the waist but didn't bother with the arms this time; it was too time-consuming.

Graham's torso went into a black refuse bag, with another two pounds of lime powder, and Dennis stored it with Howlett's remains in the wardrobe. The legs went into a different bag, which he stowed in the tea chest in his lounge. Once all the flesh and facial hair had been boiled from the head, he stashed the skull in the same bag where Johnny Howlett's skull was, also in the wardrobe in his bedroom.

It was after four o'clock on Saturday morning when he had finally completed the demanding task of covering up his latest heinous crime; victim number eleven.

Dennis ran a hot bath and cleaned himself up thinking, *You simply cannot stop this, can you? It might be time to turn yourself in to the police, Des. You're a dysfunctional man.*

Getting out of the bath at sunrise, he looked at his scrawny body in the mirror. He had lost a lot of weight since he had moved into the Cranley Gardens flat.

Stressful to be a serial killer, isn't it? he thought in revulsion.

CHAPTER 21

By January 1983, Dennis Nilsen had to deal with the stench of rotting flesh once more. And this time there was no backyard to make a bonfire in. Although he kept on adding lime powder to the body parts in the black plastic bags, the foul smell kept on lingering at 23 Cranley Gardens Street.

He bought a dozen air freshener cans at the grocery store and, after spraying half of them out in the wardrobe with the body parts, he left the empty cans on top of the bags. It disguised the decomposing odour somewhat, but couldn't mask it completely. *Oh well*, Nilsen thought, *that's as good as it's going to get*. Then he fed Bleep and went to bed. It was January 25th.

January 26th was an unusual day in London. Citizens were astounded to wake up to "red rain" that was falling all across the United Kingdom, caused by red sand from the Sahara Desert in the droplets. It was an icy Wednesday and Nilsen went to work like he did on any other Wednesday in winter, wearing his warmest coat over his suit.

Upon returning to his flat, a little after five o'clock in the afternoon, the red drizzle was still around and when he closed his umbrella to enter through the door on the ground floor, he was confronted by an elderly female tenant with purple-white candyfloss hair and a wrinkled face.

"You are Dennis Nilsen, right?" she said in a croaky voice. "The one in the attic flat?"

"Y-yes, M-ma'am," Dennis stuttered. He didn't know the old lady's name but he had seen her before and – according to his recollection – she was living in the flat below his.

"What is that smell coming from your place?" she asked, leaning on her bamboo cane, hunched like a question mark in her thick woollen jumper.

Dennis gave a fake sigh. "Oh, it's just mold. I've been trying to get rid of it, but with all this rain…" He shrugged his shoulders. "It's difficult with the moisture levels, you know?"

The elderly lady pointed upward with a pale, bunion-covered little hand and said, "That doesn't smell like mold to me, young man. I have been around long enough to know the smell of mold. That odor coming from your place smells like you're cooking venison stew and leaving it in the pot for weeks."

"I can assure you that is not the case, Ma'am," Dennis replied, smiling. "I'm real sorry about the smell. I have no idea why it stinks like that, but I will ask the landlord to come and take a look at the problem, all right?"

"Very well, then," said the woman. She brushed past him on her way out and opened her umbrella. "You have yourself a good evening now, see?"

Waving a hand, Dennis replied, "You too, Ma'am. Let's hope the red rain clears up soon." But she didn't seem to hear his response. She was already making her way across the street.

He wiped his brow with his coat's sleeve, walked inside and closed the door behind him.

What am I going to do? he thought while walking up the stairs. *Other people are also going to start to complain about the smell if I don't get rid of it soon… Damn it!*

After spraying some more air freshener in the wardrobe and opening all the windows, he decided to go for supper at the *Royal George* pub in Goslett Yard. He had seen an advertisement in the newspaper that morning about a half price special they had on black pudding.

The *Royal George* was named and designed after the *HMS Royal George*, which was a flagship vessel for the Royal English Navy back in the 1800's. The front of the pub had been designed to look like the rear of the vessel. Unlike many other pubs in London, there was a quiet atmosphere inside.

Dennis entered and chose a booth beside the front windows before ordering a pint of beer and a large dish of black pudding. He sat in silence and contemplated his life. The thought of turning himself in at a police station had been crossing his mind often lately. Now that the old lady had confronted him about the smell in his flat, he was even more determined to put a stop to his murderous behavior. The tricky part was that he didn't know how to control his subconscious urge to kill. It was almost as if he was *addicted* to taking other people's lives.

His food and beer arrived and he enjoyed it alone while pondering some more. Staring out the window, he noticed that the red drizzle had finally stopped. He was relieved; the red rain made him think of Johnny Howlett's blood in his bathtub, ten months ago.

"Hello there," a soft voice said, just as he finished the last bit of his black pudding.

Dennis looked up and saw that the voice belonged to a good-looking man, somewhere in his early twenties, with bleached blond hair and droopy eyes. He was short, maybe five-foot-five, and he was wearing a black leather jacket with a blue-and-white football scarf and black jeans.

"Hello back at you," said Dennis. "Can I help you with anything?"

"I'm Stephen," the young man told him. "Do you mind if I sit down?"

"Not at all," replied Dennis. His emotions shuddered inside his chest. *Another Stephen?* he thought. *What a rare coincidence.* It was more than four years ago when he had strangled and drowned Stephen Holmes, his very first victim.

The new Stephen took a seat across from him and Dennis said, "I'm Des Nilsen... Stephen?"

"Sinclair," Stephen clarified, rubbing his hands together. "But I was actually born Stephen Neil Guild. My biological parents rejected me and then I was adopted by the Sinclairs when I was two years old. They threw me out when I was thirteen and handed me over to social services."

"So, what can I do for you, Stephen Sinclair?" Dennis asked.

"This is kind of embarrassing, but I haven't eaten all day and I have no money left. Would you be so kind as to buy me a portion of fish and chips?"

Dennis pursed his lips, thinking. He had enough cash on him to buy the lad a meal but it was cold in the pub, since there was no fire burning in the fireplace beside the bar counter. He wanted to go home.

"Where do you live?" he asked his new acquaintance.

"I don't actually have a permanent place," Stephen said, blushing. "I stay in Salvation Army youth hostels whenever I can find one with an open space for me."

"Why don't you come back to my place?" Dennis requested. "It's in Muswell Hill, on Cranley Gardens Street, and much warmer than in here. I was on my way out in any event. I don't have much in the kitchen this late in the month, but I can buy you a burger or something on the way there."

After Stephen Sinclair had accepted the offer and thanked him, Dennis paid the bill and they left the pub. Before taking the underground tube to Highgate Station, he bought Stephen a Big Mac at a McDonalds on Oxford street, right next to the Salvation Army's headquarters.

When they arrived at his flat, Dennis Nilsen found himself embarrassed for the first time in years. While Stephen asked questions about Bleep, Nilsen was answering vaguely, staring at the inside of his chaotic home. The kitchen area was messy, the furniture in the lounge looked old and derelict, and the vulgar smell of death and decay had returned, despite all the open windows.

"Pardon the smell," he told Stephen, while closing the windows. He pointed at a dirty corner on one of the attic flat's sloped ceilings. "I don't know what kind of mold it is, but it smells like a rat or something died in here." He sprayed some air freshener in the front lounge and then switched on the electric fireplace in the bedroom. "This will heat the place up in no time," he assured his guest.

"Anything's better than living on the streets," Stephen Sinclair confessed. "This is luxury to me, especially in winter. Last night I had to sleep on a bench in Goslett Yard. Nearly froze my balls off."

Nilsen went into the kitchenette and said, "Switch on the telly. Make yourself comfortable."

After Stephen muttered a "Thank you," he switched the television on and then sank down in a dusty armchair with Bleep curled up on his lap.

"Rum or whiskey?" Nilsen called from the kitchenette. He removed his tie and dropped it into a brass bowl on the kitchen table, then took out two glasses from the small cabinet beside the fridge.

"I'll have a whiskey, cheers," Stephen replied, giving a thumbs up.

Nilsen handed him a stiff Scotch on the rocks a minute later and sat down on another armchair beside him. The programme airing on BBC2 was an episode of *Boys from the Blackstuff*, a story about five unemployed men in Liverpool and one of Nilsen's favorite shows.

"We have to watch this, Stephen," he said, rising to his feet and turning up the volume. "It's a fantastic programme! Have you seen it before?"

"Not that I can recall, but I will take your word for it. It looks pretty interesting."

Bleep jumped from Stephen's lap to the floor and started barking sharply. Dennis picked her up and said, "Do you want to stretch your legs, girl?" Then he let her out and closed the door.

"Isn't she going to freeze to death, Des?" Stephen asked in a concerned tone.

"Don't worry," Dennis replied, "she's not going outside. She likes to walk up and down the stairs and into the foyer on the ground floor. I will let her back in when the show is over." He sat down again and sipped on his drink, watching the television intensely.

Halfway through the episode, Stephen excused himself to "go to the bathroom". Upon walking the short distance to the bathroom, Dennis

Nilsen noticed that he had an aluminium tin in his one hand. Working with homeless people – many of them drug addicts – every day of his life, Nilsen instantly recognized the object. It was a tin which heroin addicts used to store their needles, opioids and other drug paraphernalia in. *So that's why he doesn't have any money for food. He's an addict – a bloody junkie. He's going to the bathroom to shoot up heroin.*

Whilst Stephen was busy shooting up in the bathroom, Dennis poured more drinks and continued watching his favorite show. Tonight's episode focussed on the character of Yosser Hughes, with his witty comments such as "Gizza' job!" ("Give us a job.")

"Stephen, are you all right in there?" Dennis called somewhere during the programme, but he got caught up in the show again before his guest could answer.

By the time the episode was finished, Stephen had returned from the bathroom and had passed out in the armchair. His head was cocked to the side in an uncomfortable position.

Dennis switched off the television and let Bleep back inside. Then he put one of his favorite vinyl records, *Tommy: The Rock Opera* on his record player, and listened to it through his headphones, sitting cross-legged on the carpet. He drank another five doubles while doing so.

Somewhere after eleven o'clock that night, Dennis got to his feet and approached Stephen Sinclair.

He cautiously touched the man's upper leg and whispered, "Stephen, are you awake?"

Stephen did not respond and Dennis Nilsen thought, *Oh, man, here we go again.* His heart was pounding in his chest while he stared at Stephen's face. "All that beauty," he said, shaking his head. "All that potential and, yet, you have to suffer from the pain of being a heroin addict."

He used his index finger and thumb to carefully open one of Stephen's eyelids. There was no reflex. He took hold of Stephen Sinclair's left wrist and raised his arm, then let go again. The arm flopped back onto his lap. Sinclair was out cold from the heroin fix earlier.

Dennis casually walked to the kitchenette and retrieved a piece of rope from the cupboard drawer below the water heater. Figuring that it was too short, he fetched his tie from the brass bowl on the kitchen table and made a ligature by securing the rope to the necktie with a fisherman's knot (the way Grandpa had taught him when he was a little boy in Aberdeenshire).

He returned to where Stephen Sinclair was propped up on the armchair and removed the scarf from the young man's neck. Then Dennis knelt down beside the chair and took a deep breath. He positioned the ligature around Stephen's throat and pulled it tight for what seemed to be an eternity. Stephen awoke from his drug-induced stupor but he was too weak to defend himself. His hands went up to his throat for a few brief moments and then his motor neurons ceased to work. He stopped breathing soon after that and then his heartbeat faded away like mist on a spring morning.

Once he was dead, Dennis began to undress him, noticing that the front part of his jeans were soaked in urine. Upon taking off the leather jacket, he saw that both Stephen's wrists were covered in dirty crepe bandages. When he removed the bandages, he found deep razor slash marks on the wrists; most probably as a result of a recent suicide attempt, Dennis reckoned.

"See, I rescued you from a nightmare," he told the lifeless corpse. "You were beyond redemption, dear Stephen, but everything is going to be all right now, you'll see." His thoughts were quite different, though. *This was one too many, Des*, he silently told himself. *Why couldn't you just leave him alone? It was* his *decision to become a drug addict, not yours. Why did you have to kill him?*

Three minutes later, Dennis Nilsen stood back and studied the nude body while smoking a cigarette. The skin was pale and hairless, barring a triangle of ginger pubic curls, and the face looked peaceful. To Nilsen, the macabre scene in front of him was more beautiful than in his wildest dreams.

Picking up the body, he took it into the bathroom and washed it in the bathtub with soap and warm water. After struggling to get the slippery corpse out of the bath, he dried it and carried it to his bedroom where he laid it on top of the bed.

Then Dennis stripped naked and lay down beside the naked dead man.

He noticed in the mirror that Stephen Sinclair's body was much paler than his own, so he got up and applied talcum powder to his skin to make them look more similar. Then he climbed back into the bed and spooned behind the corpse, staring at their nude bodies in the mirror with content for a few minutes.

His intention was to masturbate, but he couldn't get an erection. The foul smell, coming from the wardrobe with the mutilated body parts, was strongly diminishing any feelings of sexual arousal. However, Dennis Nilsen did not care at that moment. Just the feeling of someone else's soft skin against his was enough.

He had somebody to keep him company once again.

After switching off the lamp on the bedside table, he pulled the blankets over them and hugged the body of his latest victim tightly. Then he turned the cadaver's head toward him, kissed the cold forehead and said, "Goodnight, Stephen. Sleep tight, I'll see you in the morning, okay?"

Dennis fell asleep, thinking that he had completed a full circle. It was never his intention to murder so many people, but the circle was complete.

He had started with Stephen Holmes in the Melrose Avenue apartment and now he had killed Stephen Sinclair here at Cranley Gardens.

Stephen to Stephen; a full circle.

Twelve lives ruined…

CHAPTER 22

The following morning, he folded Stephen Sinclair's clothes and packed it away in his wardrobe – the one without the body parts. Then he dressed the corpse in some of his own clothes and covered it with the blanket once more. He would deal with the problem later. He had to get to the office.

He was suffering from a seriously bad hangover, but his work was a priority. He was the Executive Officer at Manpower Services – a very important man.

After a bath and a quick instant coffee, he said goodbye to Bleep and made his way to the Job Center in Kentish Town.

That afternoon, following a long day at the office, he went for drinks at the gay-friendly *King Willy* pub in Hampstead. He didn't meet anybody interesting, so he moved on to the *Sir Richard Steele* pub near the Belsize Park tube station, where he spent about an hour and a half chatting to two transvestites from Brighton. He bought them drinks and they boasted about their sexy outfits. Upon removing his wig, one of them looked strikingly similar to Billy Sutherland, Dennis Nilsen's fourth victim.

He left the *Richard Steele* pub just before ten o'clock in the evening.

When he arrived at the Belsize Park tube station to take the underground train back to Muswell Hill, the place was closed and crawling with cops and police vehicles. Barricade tape with the words POLICE LINE \ DO NOT CROSS was stretched across the entrance.

Dennis cautiously approached one of the uniformed officers and said, "Good evening, Constable. What is going on here? Why is the tube station closed off?"

The constable, a chubby man in his mid-thirties, gave a forced smile. "We have arrested a very dangerous criminal tonight; one we have been chasing after for quite some time." The perpetrator he was talking about was a man by the name of David Martin, a career criminal who would cross Nilsen's path in about two years, he would later learn in jail.

He took a cab back to his flat and poured himself a whiskey nightcap before settling on a lazy chair in his bedroom, listening to a music record: *Famous Last Words* by the popular band Supertramp. Between two of the songs, he turned to face Stephen Sinclair's corpse on the bed and said, in an upbeat tone of voice, "You know what, Stephen? You're a lot better off than that bastard they have arrested down at the tube station tonight."

***

During the last weekend of January 1983, Dennis dissected Stephen's body in the bathroom, but he was now experiencing the same dilemma he had at Melrose Avenue: he was running out of space.

While Stephen Sinclair's skull was boiling in the pasta pot on the gas stove, Dennis was carving away at the headless torso, drinking rum, smoking cigarettes and crying. "Why can't you stop this stupid act of strangling people?" he asked himself aloud, glaring at the severed legs and the torso, which was now cut in half below the ribcage. "You are such a dumb son of a bitch, Des. Look at this utter mess now. Where the hell are you going to put all these body parts?"

The answer was nothing but gruesome.

There was still some space left in the tea chest in the lounge, where he bundled the upper torso into (with arms still intact), after he'd wrapped it in newspapers. The lid of the chest could barely close and he had to sit on it and wiggle his body to seal it shut.

Upon returning to the bathroom, he still had to deal with the lower part of the torso, as well as the bulky legs. The tea chest was filled to the brim, the wardrobe was full and he didn't have anywhere else to stow these body parts. The flat was crammed with furniture and the kitchen cabinets were too small to handle the size of the legs and the pelvis. He regretted burning the portable cupboards on his last bonfire at

Melrose Avenue. They would have been perfect to solve his current conundrum.

Slumping down to the floor, his hand suddenly came into contact with a cold metal surface on the side of the bath. Dennis turned and stared at the steel insert. Up to that moment he had believed the panel was there to allow easy access to the tub's plumbing system, but now – as he knocked on it with his knuckle – he realized it was a drawer beneath the bathtub.

He slid his fingers in under the bottom part of the steel panel and pulled. The drawer came out with a screeching sound and it reminded Dennis of those rolling drawers he had seen in morgues on the movies. The size of this drawer beneath the tub was much smaller, but big enough to host the two legs and the pelvis of the corpse. He quickly shoved these body parts into the opening and kicked it shut before vomiting into the toilet bowl.

After he had scrubbed the bathroom floor with bleach, he took a long bath and then dressed in tracksuit pants and a thick woollen jersey. He smoked another cigarette in the lounge and then took Bleep for a walk around the block. Stephen Sinclair's head was still boiling on the stove.

While strolling down the street, racking his brain about what to do with the third skull in his Cranley Gardens flat, a thought came to Dennis. Before he had stashed Graham Allan's legs in the tea chest, the chest had not been empty. He now recalled there was a soccer ball inside and he had never taken it out; it was still there, underneath the leg bones. It was a ball he had bought at a game between Liverpool and Manchester United about six years earlier.

A bloody soccer ball! his mind told him. *A soccer ball the size of a human head!*

He rushed back to his flat and switched off the stove before pouring himself another rum and Coke. While waiting for the water in the pot to cool down, he sat down at the kitchen table and leafed through the Sunday paper to establish whether anything had been published about a missing youth named Stephen Sinclair. There was nothing of the sorts, so he decided he was nearly out of the woods. He just had to replace the soccer ball in the chest with the boiled skull and spray some more air freshener. Problem solved.

When the water had cooled down to room temperature, he drained the frothy liquid from the pot and took out the skull. Then he went into the lounge, unpacked the tea chest and removed the soccer ball. He rearranged everything inside – Graham Allan's legs and Stephen Sinclair's upper torso and arms – and added the skull. This time he didn't have to sit on the chest to close it properly.

Relieved, he wiped sweat from the back of his neck and placed the soccer ball in a carton box in the corner of the lounge. Bleep was looking at him with big eyes.

***

Just over a week later, on Friday, February 4th 1983, Dennis Nilsen's real troubles started.

As he returned home from the office, one of the other tenants at Cranley Gardens walked out and struck up a conversation with him. He recognized her as the ground floor tenant who lived there with her boyfriend. He couldn't recall her name but he thought it was something like Fiona or Felicity.

"Are you also experiencing problems with your lavatory?" she asked, frowning.

"Not that I know of," Dennis replied, biting his fingernails. "Why?"

"Our's doesn't want to flush," she told him. "I don't know if there's a burst pipe somewhere, or whether it has something to do with the strike."

Dennis knew all about the water-workers' strike in London at the time. Many areas were without water and standpipes were in use for public supplies.

"Since when have you had the issue?" he inquired. He could hear the tremble in his voice.

"Last night it was still working, but this morning it appeared to be blocked."

Telling her that he will check on his toilet right away, Dennis hurried up the stairs and into his flat.

When he sat down at the kitchen table, he shared his thoughts with Bleep: "Listen, girl, if all the other residents are experiencing problems with the drainage system and we are not, the landlord might come up here for an inspection. We have to make a plan. Better safe than sorry, right?"

He thought about it for a while, then grabbed a notepad from the lounge and wrote a letter to the landlord, complaining that his drain was blocked and that that the situation for both himself and the other tenants at the property was becoming intolerable. He posted the letter in the letterbox downstairs and received an answer the next morning:

Dear Mr Nilsen,

We fully understand the frustration and we are sorry for the inconvenience. We have contacted the plumbing company but, unfortunately, due to it being the weekend and because of the water strike, they will only be able to send someone out on Tuesday afternoon.

We hope this is in order.

Sincerely,

The board of trustees, 23 Cranley Gardens, Muswell Hill.

Dennis Nilsen enjoyed the rest of the weekend without worrying too much about the tenants in the ground floor apartment. It seemed that his drainage system worked fine, but that it clogged the pipes of the apartments further down.

***

The plumber responded on Tuesday, February 8th.

Opening a drain cover at the side of the house, he climbed down the twelve-foot shaft and discovered the drain was blocked, but not by the usual mess of hair and napkins. It was packed with a rotting, flesh-like substance and numerous small bones of unknown origin. The stench coming from the obstructed sewer pipe was unbearable. This alarmed the plumber to such a degree that he reported his concerns to his supervisor. Because he had only arrived at the property at dusk, the plumber and his supervisor agreed to postpone any further investigation into the blockage until the next morning.

Before he left the property, the plumber convened with some of the tenants to show them what he had found and to discuss the source of the substance. The elderly lady on the second floor was on vacation, so he spoke to Dennis and the woman and her boyfriend from the ground floor apartment.

When the plumber speculated about how similar the substance was in appearance to human flesh, Dennis replied: "It looks to me like someone has been flushing down their Kentucky Fried Chicken."

"Did any of you flush dog-meat down the drain?" the plumber asked.

The other tenants shook their heads and Dennis said, "I have a dog, but she feeds on tinned meat." Then he stuck his hands in his pockets and asked, "How are you going to clear this mess?"

"We have a special plumbing suction machine, but we will only be able to do it tomorrow morning."

The plumber finally left the property and Dennis Nilsen gave a nervous sigh of relief behind his hand. He was a worried man. For five years he'd been operating underneath the radar and now he was about to be exposed in a bright spotlight.

That evening, he went to the closest Kentucky outlet to buy some chicken. His plan was to replace the flesh the plumber had found with pieces of fried chicken. However, he was too late. In those days, the takeout restaurants didn't stay open that late and when he arrived at the outlet at 7:15 p.m. it was already closed.

Nilsen went back home with a heavy heart and waited until after midnight before he went outside and into the manhole, carrying a flashlight and a plastic bag.

He picked out all the pieces of flesh he could find and put them in the plastic carrier bag. After about twenty minutes, he thought he had cleared up most of the evidence and he exited the manhole to dump the bag of human flesh behind the back garden hedge of the property. What Dennis Nilsen didn't know at the time, was that one of the tenants at 25 Cranley Gardens, the building next door, was studying him through her window…

***

Back in his flat, he washed his hands and arms and stood in the bathroom, staring at his seemingly hollow eye sockets in the dirty mirror, thinking about what to do next. Glancing at his wristwatch, he noticed that it was already way past one o'clock in the morning.

There was no time left to get rid of the body parts inside his flat, so he decided to go to bed and hope for the best. The way the next day was going to pan out was almost like a gamble for him by then. He was in two minds about everything that's been going on. He didn't want to go to prison, but he also didn't want to carry on living the life he had been living.

If they catch me, they catch me, he silently told himself. *I've had enough. I cannot take this anymore.*

One of the thoughts that had crossed his mind earlier was suicide, but he didn't know how. He didn't have a long or strong enough rope, and no strong medication to overdose on. He certainly wasn't going to cut himself. The thought of all that blood made the hair stand up on the back of his neck.

Dennis felt sick to his stomach when he climbed into bed at quarter to two.

"Bleep, who is going to look after you when they come for me?" he asked his dog before switching off the bedside lamp.

At 7:30 a.m. the following morning, when Dennis had already left for work, the plumber returned to 23 Cranley Gardens to find that the drain had been cleared by someone. Naturally, this aroused even more suspicion and he once again informed his supervisor, who called the police.

While waiting for the police to arrive, the plumber discovered some other pieces of flesh and four small bones in a pipe, leading from the drain which was linked to the top floor of the house. When he inspected the bones, he thought they looked as if they originated from a person's hand – not the fingers, but the slender bones in the upper part of the hand.

The police arrived half an hour later and found even more small bones and scraps of what looked like either human or animal flesh, in the same pipe coming from the attic flat's drain. These remains were taken to the mortuary at Hornsey, where a pathologist did some tests and informed the police that the pieces of flesh were of human origin.

That afternoon, minutes before Dennis Nilsen left the office in Kentish Town, he told one of his colleagues: "If I'm not in tomorrow, I am either ill, dead, or in jail."

He knew he was at the fifty-ninth minute of the eleventh hour. He told himself that he wouldn't be surprized if the cops were waiting for him when he arrived home.

CHAPTER 23

When he returned home a few minutes after five o'clock on Wednesday afternoon, February 9th, 1983, Dennis Nilsen knew it was finally the end of the road for him. A shiver, colder than the late winter chill, ran down his spine when he noticed two police vehicles behind the plumber's panel van in front of 23 Cranley Gardens. A Detective Chief Inspector and two of his colleagues in plainclothes were waiting outside the entrance to the three-storey building.

As Dennis walked up the pathway in the snow, the sounds of the neighborhood increased his anxiety: dogs barking, kids yelling, and cars buzzing in his ears.

"Mr Nilsen?" said the detective, raising his brow. He had curly black hair and broad shoulders; quite an imposing figure, standing at six-foot-three in his police uniform and long overcoat.

Dennis looked down at his shoes. "Yes, that's me." By now, he was so thin that his blazer, which once fitted him perfectly, hung over his upper body like a tent.

The detective introduced himself and his colleagues, after which he stated: "We have come to question you about the drain blockage in the building."

"Why would a policeman concern himself with drains?" Dennis asked. He pointed at the detective's two colleagues. "Are they health inspectors?"

"No, Mr Nilsen," replied the detective, "they are not health inspectors. They are also police officers. Will you escort us up to your flat in order for us to discuss the matter further?"

Keeping his mouth shut, Dennis opened the front door and began to climb the stairs to his flat's door. The police officers followed him in a single file, also staying quiet.

When they entered the flat, it was freezing inside. Despite the snow, all the windows were wide open. Everybody could smell the odour of rotting flesh, even with the breeze blowing through the open windows. Dennis frowned and said to the detective, "Sir, you haven't told me why the police would be interested in my drains."

Placing his hands on his hips, the detective replied, "Mr Nilsen, the building's drains are blocked with human remains."

"Good grief, how awful!" Dennis exclaimed, trying to sound bewildered. "Where did it come from?"

"From your flat, Mr Nilsen. I'm sure I don't have to tell *you* anything about that."

Dennis sunk into one of his armchairs and said, "No, you're right, Detective, you don't have to."

His heart was in his mouth. After all these years he had finally been caught. He had been on the right side of the law for a long time, during his army years and his short career as a policeman, but in the past five years he had been a vicious criminal. He was on the wrong side of the law now and he understood that he was in big trouble. Everything was now going to come to an end.

As if she knew her master was going to be taken away soon, Bleep jumped onto his lap and squeaked.

The detective suddenly raised his voice and demanded: "Don't mess about, Nilsen, where is the rest of the body?"

A strange tranquillity washed over Dennis and he couldn't believe the calmness in his voice when he replied, "In two plastic bags in that wardrobe." He pointed at the bedroom with his chin.

"Is there anything else you want to tell us?" asked one of the officers.

"It's a long story," Dennis told him. "It goes back a long time." He gave a loud sigh. "I will tell you everything. It just sort of happened. I want to get it off my chest but not here, at the police station."

The detective pulled on a pair of latex gloves, walked into the bedroom and cautiously inspected the contents of the black refuse bags in the wardrobe while covering his nose and mouth with one hand. One of the bags contained two dissected torsos, and a smaller shopping bag filled with a number of internal organs. Several cans of air fresheners were scattered around the bags. The second bag contained a human skull, almost completely devoid of flesh, a severed head, and a torso with the arms attached but the hands missing.

"What the hell?" the detective said, gasping. He turned and glared at Dennis.

"I know," Dennis replied solemnly. He lifted Bleep from his lap and carefully put her down on the carpet. Then he stood up and held his hands behind his back.

The detective slapped a pair of cold stainless steel handcuffs around his wrists. "Dennis Andrew Nilsen, I am hereby arresting you on suspicion of murder. You will now come with us to Hornsey Police Station, where your rights will be explained to you and where you will be interrogated by a team of police investigators. Do you understand?"

Nodding his head in comprehension, Dennis mumbled, "Will you please arrange for someone to look after my dog while I'm at the station?" One of the police officers picked Bleep up, covered her in a blanket and carried her outside.

Once Dennis Nilsen was inside the police car, on the backseat, the detective said, "The human remains in your flat, how many bodies are we talking about? Two or three?"

Nilsen, sweating profusely, stared out of the window and replied, "Three. But it's much worse than that. Probably more than a dozen since 1978. I will tell you everything." He sighed again. "You know, if you haven't caught me today, it would have most likely ended in hundreds of bodies."

He didn't hear the detective's incredulous response. He was thinking about his crimes. *Only* you *screwed up your life, Des Nilsen. Not Grandpa, not the boy who saved you from drowning, and not the Arab taxi driver who tried to kill you in Yemen. You did all of this to yourself. You've become addicted to killing people and you know what? It is too late for remorse now. You need to pay for your sins, you sick psychopath.*

Thirteen minutes later, when the police car rolled through the gates of Hornsey Police Station, he was still thinking. *Where would young Stephen Holmes be today if you haven't ripped the life from his body, Des? And what about the aspiring Kenneth Ockenden? Or Johnny Howlett? You have aimlessly ended these people's lives without thinking what they could have achieved, you son of a bitch.*

***

An hour after that, Dennis found himself in a smoke-filled room with beige walls and a green linoleum floor with no windows. He was sitting on a plastic chair, behind a government-issued wooden table. On the other side of the table stood two police officers, behind two more white plastic chairs. The one was the detective with the broad shoulders who had arrested him earlier and the other one was a stocky uniformed officer with a brush cut hairstyle, a thick brown moustache, and a fake tanned skin. Both of them were drinking black coffee from Styrofoam cups and the officer with the brush cut was casually dragging on a Chesterfield filter cigarette.

Earlier, Dennis had been processed – photographs taken, fingerprints recorded, his rights explained, and documents completed – and now the handcuffs had been removed from his wrists. He was relieved; the handcuffs made him anxious and jittery.

The officer with the brush cut spoke first. "Mr Nilsen, would you like legal counsel to be present while you speak to us?" he asked loudly.

"No, I'm fine for now," replied Dennis.

"Would you like some coffee?"

"No, thanks," Dennis declined, shaking his head slowly. He stared at the officer and said, "May I ask you for a cigarette, please?"

The officer retrieved a packet of Chesterfields and a disposal lighter from his jacket's inner pocket. Sliding the two items over the table, he sat down and said, "Mr Nilsen, we are recording this interview to be used as evidence at a later stage. Do you have any objection to that?"

Dennis lit a cigarette, inhaled, and then replied, "I guess I don't have a choice, so go ahead."

A clerk came in with a tape recorder and placed it in the middle of the table. The police officer pressed the record button and then said, "You're a civil servant, right?"

"Yes."

"In which department?"

"Unemployment," Dennis answered. "I work in a job center for Manpower Services."

"You assured us that you would tell us everything about your crimes, so please go ahead."

Dennis grimaced. "Where do you want me to begin?" *What on earth do I tell them?* he thought. *Do I give them names? Do I give them all the details? Where am I to start?*

"Explain to us about the dismembered body parts in your flat at Cranley Gardens."

Blowing smoke out through his nose, Dennis said, "How do you mean? In what context?"

"Well, how the body parts came to be there," the officer clarified, clearly irritated with his suspect's arrogance and laidback attitude.

"Did you search the rest of the flat?" Dennis asked in a low voice. *Yes, that's right, Des,* his mind told him. *Rather give them all the details. Come clean now and they might take it easier on you during your trial... Man, you are in deep, deep in trouble now.*

The interrogating officer frowned. "Why?"

"There are some more human remains in my tea chest in the lounge and in the drawer under the bath."

Both police officers flinched.

Dennis Nilsen continued to provide them with extensive details about his killing spree, starting at Melrose Avenue in 1978, confessing to murdering a dozen men or more. He also admitted to having unsuccessfully attempted to kill a number of other people, who had either escaped or, on one occasion, had been at the brink of death but had been revived and allowed to leave his home. At no point did he show any remorse and he appeared to be quite eager to assist the police with the evidence against him. The information about the unsuccessful murders were especially helpful, since it was effectively leading investigators to live witnesses.

At a stage during the interview, the detective stopped Dennis in mid-sentence and said, "Will you accompany us to your previous home at 195 Melrose Avenue tomorrow afternoon?"

"Sure," Dennis agreed, "but there is not much to see there."

"What will we find at the property?" asked the detective, interlocking his fingers on the table.

Rolling his eyes, Dennis said, "Unless the site has been cleared by contractors you will only find some bone ash at the back of the garden." He stubbed his cigarette out in a glass ashtray, cleared his throat and then said, "May I please have a glass of water?"

The bulky detective got up and poured water from a dispenser against the wall into a Styrofoam cup. "Here you go," he muttered, placing the cup in front of Dennis on the table. Dennis drank half of it and then said, "Thank you, sir."

The officer with the brush cut lit another cigarette and sat back in his chair. "Mr Nilsen, help us to understand this, please? Tell us what started you off in 1978?"

What started me off? Dennis thought, biting his lower lip. "You know," he finally said, "that is something I have never stopped asking myself. There is no disputing the fact that I am a violent killer under certain circumstances. I know it would have been better if my reason for killing was sex, bloodlust or sadism. But it is none of these. I was hoping you would be able to tell me why I did it."

"Why didn't you stop after the first victim?"

Dennis took a deep breath. "I don't know."

"Did you deliberately lure young men to your home to kill them?"

"What do you want me to say?" Dennis answered. He drank some more water.

"Did you intend to kill all of these people, Mr Nilsen?"

"What I did seemed right at the time."

"Wait, are you saying that you've had a need to kill?"

"In some cases," Dennis Nilsen said, "at that precise moment of the act, I felt my sole reason for existence was to carry out the act. Killing others gave me a reason to live. There is no other way to explain it. It just happened."

"Unbelievable," replied the detective, shuddering.

While the interview was taking place, a Detective Superintendent Chambers accompanied two other police officers to Cranley Gardens, where the plastic bags with the body parts were removed from the wardrobe in the bedroom and taken to Hornsey Mortuary for examination.

In a follow-up interview, conducted on the morning of February 10th, Nilsen confessed that the dismembered body parts in his flat at Cranley Gardens were from the corpses of three men, all of whom he had killed by some form of strangulation, he explained, thereby implicating himself beyond a shadow of a doubt in these murders.

This presented a dilemma for the police.

Usually they would find a dead body and begin to search for the killer from that point onward. In this case, they had a killer of at least twelve people, with no corpses and only a few body parts. They realized they had to move into reverse engineering mode.

That afternoon, the police went back to 23 Cranley Gardens where they found the lower section of a torso and two legs stowed in the bathroom drawer underneath the tub, as well as a skull, a section of a torso, and various bones in the tea chest in the lounge.

On the same day, Nilsen accompanied the police to Melrose Avenue, where he showed them the three locations – one in the rear garden and two at the dumpsite behind the property – where he had burned the remains of his victims on bonfires. The snow had stopped and the sun had come out, but there was a cold wind blowing through Cricklewood.

"How many people did you burn on these so-called bonfires?" asked one of the police officers.

Dennis Nilsen rubbed his chin, thinking. A feeling of nostalgia washed over him as he looked at the site where he had made his bonfires. After a while, he pushed his glasses up the bridge of his nose and said, "On the first fire, only one… Stevie. But the other two were genuine bonfires; big ones. Probably another nine to twelve bodies, I can't be sure."

"You can't be sure?" the police officer exclaimed. "What does that mean?"

"It means exactly what I told you, sir," Dennis replied. The icy wind was blowing his hair into his eyes and he threw his head back. "That I'm not sure how many people's lives I took during the timespan of five years."

"You arrogant bastard!" shouted the officer.

***

Over the following thirty-six hours, police investigators found over a thousand human bone fragments behind the property, most of them blackened and charred by fire. Using these fragments, they had to somehow work backward and figure out the identities of the victims.

Two days later, the story was on the front page of the *Daily Mirror* newspaper, which reported that Dennis Nilsen had been formally charged with the murder of his last victim, Stephen Sinclair.

Under English law, the police only had forty-eight hours in which to charge Nilsen, or else they had to release him. Assembling the remains of the victims killed at Cranley Gardens in the Hornsey Mortuary, the coroner – with the help of a pathologist – was able to confirm that the fingerprints on one of the remaining hands matched those of Stephen Sinclair on police files. Nilsen was charged with the murder of Sinclair and a statement revealing this was released to the press. Journalists soon began to refer to Dennis Nilsen as the "British Jeffrey Dahmer".

A team of police investigators interviewed Nilsen on sixteen separate occasions over the next four days, in sessions that totalled audio recordings of more than thirty hours. These audio recordings revealed some bizarre confessions.

With most victims he masturbated as he knelt over the bodies and Nilsen also admitted to having occasionally engaged in intercrural sex with his victims' bodies.

When asked why the heads found at Cranley Gardens had been subjected to moist heat (as per the pathologist's report), he confessed that he had boiled the heads of his victims in a large cooking pot on his gas stove, in order for the contents to disintegrate, therefor eliminating the need to dispose of the brain and flesh.

He also confirmed that, on more than one occasion, he had removed the internal organs from the victims' bodies at Melrose Avenue and placed them in bags, which he then dumped in a nearby park to be eaten by wildlife.

To a question about whether he had any remorse for his crimes, Dennis Nilsen replied: "I wished I could stop, but I just couldn't. I had no other thrill or happiness in life." He went on to say that he took no pleasure from the act of killing, but that he "worshipped the art and the act of death."

After the thirty hours of confessions, Nilsen was held at Brixton Prison, where he awaited a preliminary trial date. In the time he was there, he wrote over fifty pages of his memories to assist the prosecution in their case. In addition, he drew what he called "sad sketches", which detailed the treatment of some of his victims. There was a sketch of Kenneth Ockenden bundled up in the wardrobe, one of the lower half of Stephen Sinclair's naked dismembered torso, and one of Martyn Duffey, asleep in an armchair with his head falling to one side.

Although Nilsen appeared to be without remorse, he showed great interest in the press and the public's attitude toward him. He kept on asking the prison warden to bring him every day's newspapers, where his story was on many occasions the headline news.

According to Nilsen, upon being transferred to Brixton Prison, his mood was one of "resignation and relief", and his thoughts were that he would be seen by the public and the media – in accordance with the law – as "innocent until proven guilty."

He refused to wear a prison uniform while he was at Brixton. He told the guards that this was against his rights as a human being and in breach of prison rules. When the warden instructed the guards to take away his civilian clothes, Nilsen protested further by not wearing any clothes at all. This resulted in a rule that he was not allowed to leave his cell to go outside or into "general population" areas.

Dennis Nilsen wrote the following self-appraisal letter while he was awaiting trial in prison:

I am not trained to interpret the workings of the mind and its effect upon personality and actions.

With lay experience, my personal conclusions flow from what are only some unofficial guestimates. The experts do not know me as I know myself.

I have felt that since my teenage years that I have been a creative psychopath. Since I have committed 15 killings and probably 8 attempted killings, I feel able to go further on this self-assessment. In times of acute emotional pressure and under the triggering influence of spirits i.e. alcohol, usually dormant mental forces have been released which have made mine the actions of a destructive psychopath.

These two conditions are not strictly 'mental illness', they seem to be more 'acceptable' in law as 'gross personality defects'. I felt an overwhelming desire to kill (in cases I remember). The strong moral side of my character should have produced the strength and power to resist this. It may be that the conditions which existed at that time (and the pressures) are now gone but I cannot allow the 'buck' to travel outside my personality. Being a practised Public Servant for 23 years makes it difficult to display the weakness of open emotion.

My victims are still causing emotional pain to their surviving relatives. In my actions I can't look back - only forward. I deserve punishment for their deaths. I feared the inevitable punishment from the start. I am the cold light of day.

I knew that I had committed a grievous crime.

I could not handle the feeling of horror and shame. Afterwards I managed to suppress all thoughts of morality. In my mind I would make my peace and my feelings of genuine remorse with the body. I felt they would have forgiven me as they lay at peace. I never had any feeling of wanting to cause pain. I would abhor having to disfigure the body by the necessary act of dissection. The greater the beauty (in my estimation) of the man, the greater was the sense of loss and grief. Their dead naked bodies fascinated me but I would have done anything to have them back alive.

In at least 3 of the attempts I managed to revive them and felt like I had actually saved their lives. These successes brought great happiness to me. I could not understand why I had apparently tried to kill them in the first place. I was not actually horrified at the dead bodies but I was disgusted with my own body, that it was not dead also. I visualised my body lying dead on a mortuary slab.

I thought that death might give us what life could not and it would be forever.

Right now I feel I am able to enjoy a sexual relationship with an attractive male or female. I am perhaps now under no pressure. As an ordinary prisoner nobody now expects anything of me. I have no further need of medicinal 'booze'. My mental state now is better than in the last few years.

In many respects I have escaped from out there to in here.

Des Nilsen.

Much later, Nilsen corrected himself by saying that he hadn't killed fifteen people like he had written in his letter, but that the total number of victims he had murdered between 1978 and 1983 was, in fact, twelve.

This number was confirmed by the authorities after years of investigations. Nilsen told the police that the reason for his fabrication of the three additional victims was because of the pressure he was under, while being interviewed, as well as to "stick with the figure".

The "figure" in his mind was based on the fact that he had confessed on the site visit to Melrose Avenue that he had burned in the region of twelve bodies on his bonfires. That, plus the three at Cranley Gardens, got him stuck on the number fifteen.

He confessed that the three unidentified victims he had initially confessed to killing – an Irishman in September 1980, a hippy in November 1980, and a skinhead in April 1981 – had been invented to make his story more believable and to sound more cooperative.

The press, however, speculated widely that this number (fifteen) was fabricated to exceed the number of people the Yorkshire Ripper had murdered (thirteen).

***

The police tried their utmost best to give Bleep away to other tenants at Cranley Gardens and even advertised the Collie in local newspapers, in order to find a home for her. But, sadly, everybody said that they didn't want a serial killer's dog in their houses.

Poor Bleep was euthanized a number of days after Dennis Nilsen's arrest.

Despite being such a loyal dog for so long, she had indirectly become his last "victim".

***

On May 26th 1983, Nilsen stood in a preliminary hearing at the Old Bailey Central Criminal Court of England on five counts of murder and two of attempted murder. These were the victims the police had by then identified from the bones at Melrose Avenue and the mutilated body parts at Cranley Gardens. A sixth murder charge was later added. The two attempted murder charges related to "the ones that got away" – Carl Stottor and Paul Nobbs.

The trial date was set for October 24th.

By the time of the preliminary hearing, the story was attracting major media attention. Some of the newspapers now began to label Dennis the *Muswell Hill Killer* – ignoring the fact that most of his murders actually took place in Cricklewood and not Muswell Hill – while others called him the *Kindly Killer*, based on the notion that he always provided shelter and food for his victims before murdering them.

Dennis Nilsen fired his legal counsel after the preliminary hearing, then rehired him and fired him once again, five weeks before his murder trial started, expressing his intention to defend himself. However, a few days later he hired a new attorney to represent him.

This new lawyer convinced him to plead not guilty by reason of diminished responsibility at his upcoming trial. Initially, Dennis had intended to plead guilty to each charge of murder.

Meanwhile, the warden at Brixton Prison had his hands full with the new addition to his correctional facility. Dennis wasn't an easy prisoner to work with. He tried to make life hell for the warden and his guards.

In the first week of August, he threw the contents of his chamber pot out of his cell, hitting several prison guards. This incident resulted in him spending fifty-six days in solitary confinement.

He was released back to his cell on October 4th 1983.

CHAPTER 24

"All rise for the honourable Mr Justice Croom-Johnson!" the high bailiff's voice thundered in the main courtroom of the Old Bailey courthouse.

The people in the courtroom gallery stood up in unison, followed by Dennis Nilsen in the defense bench. He was wearing formal black trousers, a white shirt and a black jacket with no tie.

Your life is over, Des, he silently told himself, watching the judge proceed to the raised platform, while the twelve members of the jury took their places in the jury bench.

The judged ordered everyone to sit down and then opened proceedings with the usual stiffness of English court cases in the 1980s.

First to speak after the opening, was the Chief Administrator of the court.

"Dennis Andrew Nilsen," he announced, "you are charged with six counts of murder and two counts of attempted murder. In relation to these charges, how do you plead before this court?"

Dennis slowly rose to his feet, looked at the judge with confused eyes and said, "I would like to enter a plea of not guilty in relation to all eight charges, My Lord."

A number of people in the gallery started whispering words of disbelief to each other.

What they didn't know was that the defense and the prosecution had already agreed that Dennis Nilsen had killed, but the question was raised by the defense about his state of mind when he had performed these acts. While the defense attorney argued that Dennis wasn't capable of intention to commit murder – due to diminished responsibility caused by a mental defect – the prosecutor's stance was that he was in full control of his actions and that he had premeditated the murders. The defense was fighting for a conviction of manslaughter, rather than murder, and that was the reason Dennis had to plead not guilty in relation to the murder charges.

After opening statements by the prosecution and defense attorneys, Judge Croom-Johnson handed the floor to the state's counsel to call their first witness.

"The Crown calls Mr Douglas Stewart," said the prosecuting lawyer. "May it please Your Lordship."

Dennis Nilsen flinched where he was sitting in the defense bench. He instantly recognized the name. It was another one that "got away."

Douglas Stewart was sworn in and then the prosecutor asked, "In relation to the defendant, Mr Nilsen, can you please tell the court what transpired between the two of you in November 1980?"

Stewart cleared his throat and spoke into the microphone. "Certainly, sir. It was on a cold night during the second week of November when I awoke in Dennis… in Mr Nilsen's flat and my ankles were bound together with a necktie. Mr Nilsen was straddling me and he was busy strangling me around my neck with both his hands."

"What happened then?" asked the prosecutor.

"Well, I tried to defend myself. A struggle took place and, eventually, I managed to overpower him. When I ran for the door, Mr Nilsen shouted: 'Take my money! Take my money!'"

"Why do you think he said that, Mr Stewart?"

"I think," Stewart replied, looking up at the judge, "that he wanted the other tenants to hear him, so that he could later claim I was an intruder."

"Objection, My Lord!" Dennis Nilsen's defense counsel called out. "The witness is not qualified to make that statement. It's complete and utter speculation."

"Overruled," replied the judge. "The witness was a victim of an unprovoked physical attack and is entitled to his opinion. I will allow it before this court."

The prosecutor grinned and said, "Thank you, My Lord. The Crown asked the question in order to show that Mr Nilsen was acting rationally at the time, since he had the presence of mind to think about a cover story for his attack on the witness." He consulted his notes and then asked, "Mr Stewart, what happened after you escaped the flat at Cranley Gardens?"

Stewart clenched his jaw. "I reported the incident to the police right away, at the Hornsey Police Station, and they questioned Mr Nilsen the next day."

"Do you happen to know what the outcome of this questioning was?" asked the prosecutor.

"Yes, the police phoned me that evening and said that there were too many discrepancies between my testimony and Mr Nilsen's recollection of the events. They told me that they were going to dismiss the case and called it a 'lovers' quarrel'. I was furious with their ignorance."

"Thank you, Mr Stewart," said the prosecuting attorney, clasping his hands together. He turned to the judge and announced: "I have no further questions for the witness, My Lord."

Judge Croom-Johnson nodded and shifted his gaze to Nilsen's lawyer. "Your witness," he said.

The defense attorney stood up, buttoned his jacket and addressed Douglas Stewart. "Mr Stewart, what were you doing before you woke up in Mr Nilsen's flat?"

Rubbing his chin, Stewart replied in a hesitant voice: "I had dinner earlier that evening."

"Isn't it true," said the defense attorney, "that you were in fact having you so-called *dinner* in a *pub*... a pub by the name of the Pig and Whistle, and that you were consuming copious amounts of alcohol before accompanying my client to his flat?"

Stewart remained silent.

"In fact," the defense attorney continued, "you drank nine double whiskeys each and only shared a plate of chips between the two of you for *dinner*?"

"I don't think I drank that much," replied Douglas Stewart, shaking his head.

"Well, Mr Stewart, unfortunately for you, Mr Nilsen kept the receipt from that evening and the bartender confirmed that you drank nine of the seventeen double whiskeys shown on said receipt. So, wouldn't you say that you were intoxicated to a degree where you would not be able to recall exactly what happened on that night?"

When Douglas Stewart didn't offer a reply, Nilsen's attorney smiled and said, "No further questions, My Lord," without looking at the judge. He was staring at the jury and, based on the frowns on their faces, he knew he had planted the seed of reasonable doubt in their minds.

After a brief re-cross-examination of Douglas Stewart, he was excused from the witness stand and the prosecution called a university student, Paul Nobbs.

He testified about the morning when he had awoken in Nilsen's flat with a swollen face, bloodshot eyes and a burning throat. Telling the court that he suspected that Dennis Nilsen had tried to strangle him during the night, he said that he didn't report the incident to the police because he was afraid of his sexuality being discovered.

The same as with Douglas Stewart, the defense questioned the credibility of Paul Nobbs, based on the drunken stupor he had been in on the night of the alleged attack.

The prosecution's star witness turned out to be young Carl Stottor, a.k.a. Khara le Fox. He told the court in a trembling voice about the night he got tangled up in Nilsen's sleeping bag and how he came to his senses later in the bathtub filled with water.

"At first I thought he was helping me," Carl testified with watery eyes, "when he told me to stay still while I was tangled up in the sleeping bag. But later, when he was clearly trying to drown me in the bathtub,

I realized that he had tried to strangle me earlier." Carl stopped speaking for a moment and then added, "I was begging for my life, My Lord." He stared at Dennis Nilsen in the defense bench, then dropped his head in his hands and began to sob uncontrollably.

"Mr Stottor," said the judge, "please take your time. We understand that it is traumatic for you to re-create the incident in your mind, but the jury has a right to hear your testimony." He shifted his gaze from Carl Stottor to the audience in the gallery and announced: "The court will now take a five-minute break and will resume at 3:40 p.m."

After the break, Carl continued his emotional statement and ended with how Dennis Nilsen had brought him back to life later that morning and how he had taken care of him until he was strong enough to leave the apartment, three days later.

Upon cross-examination, Carl told the defense attorney that he didn't believe Dennis had taken care of him out of remorse. He said that he knew it was because Dennis felt ashamed of what he had done.

***

The next day, the Detective Chief Inspector responsible for Dennis Nilsen's arrest took the stand and gave his account of Nilsen's interviews.

"He was very matter-of-factly during our interrogation," the detective explained. "It was almost as if he wanted to build a case against himself." Shaking his head slightly, he continued: "This struck my colleagues and I as very odd. We usually see erratic behavior by people who had commit such heinous crimes. Mr Nilsen was completely forthcoming and explained to us in detail what he had done."

Looking up at the judge, the detective said, "Mr Nilsen also made several written statements to us, some of which I would like to read to the court, may it please Your Lordship."

"Please continue," the judge replied.

The detective put on his reading glasses and began to read the statement aloud:

"When under pressure of work and extreme pain of social loneliness and utter misery, I am drawn compulsively to a means of temporary escape from reality. This is achieved by taking increased amounts of alcohol and listening to stereo music, which mentally removes me to a high plane of ecstasy, joy and tears. This is a totally emotional experience... I relive experiences from childhood to present, taking out the bad bits. When I take alcohol, I see myself drawn along and moved out of my isolated, prison flat. I bring with me people who are not always allowed to leave because I want them to share my experiences and high feeling."

After the Detective Chief Inspector had read a number of these written statements, the defense counsel cross-examined him, without any success, and then he was excused from the stand.

The prosecution lawyer stood up and said, "Ladies and gentlemen of the jury, I would like you to pay close attention as the Detective Superintendent Chambers will now show you some drawings and descriptions, detailing the defendant's formal confessions to the police."

The Detective Superintendent switched on an overhead projector and began to show these images – copied to transparent plastic film – to the shocked jury.

It was like leafing through a horror picture book.

There were drawings and descriptions of Nilsen's ritualistic sexual acts, his way of dissecting the bodies and even the methods of storing the bodies under the floorboards at Melrose Avenue. These storage sketches were especially disturbing, since Dennis Nilsen had spared no detail when it came to the maggots and worms crawling from the corpses' mouths, noses and ears.

In one of the pictures, Nilsen had drawn a bonfire with flames licking at the faces of victims who were portrayed as still being alive and screaming in agony. Below the picture were the words: BONFIRE BODIES.

Sitting there with incredulous looks upon their faces, members of the jury had to withstand these gruesome images for over five hours, while the Detective Superintendent explained to them in detail how the murders, the acts of necrophilia, and the disposal of cadavers had taken place at Melrose Avenue and Cranley Gardens.

Although there was a stern look in his eyes, Dennis Nilsen watched with fascination. He became nostalgic once again as he admired his detailed sketches and captions. *You did well, Des,* his mind told him. *You have committed some serious crimes by killing those innocent men, but you did well in providing accurate recollections of your actions. Good on you, Des.*

Looking out the window, he could see how the autumn wind was swirling around reddish-brown leafs and how the swallows were preparing for their journey to the southern parts of Africa. He realized in that moment that he would never be free like again like those leafs or those swallows…

***

Over the next four days, the court listened to the thirty hours of interviews conducted by various police officers. During the playback of these audio recordings, the jury heard how Nilsen gave detailed recollections of the way in which he had lured his victims to his home, how he had strangled them, and how he had interacted with the dead bodies afterwards.

Following this marathon session, a uniformed police officer handed the Detective Superintendent five transparent plastic bags containing physical evidence.

The Detective Superintendent held up the first bulky bag and said, "My Lord, the prosecution would like to introduce to the court exhibit 16-A. This is the cooking pot in which the defendant boiled the heads of Mr John Howlett, Mr Graham Allan and Mr Stephen Sinclair."

That silenced the audience in the Old Bailey courtroom. With the names being pronounced, it seemed that everybody now visualized Nilsen's victims for the first time as real human beings.

Holding up the second bag, the Detective Superintendent Chambers announced, "The prosecution would like to introduce to the court exhibit 16-B. This is the chopping board the defendant used to dissect Mr John Howlett's body on."

He continued to introduce more physical evidence while holding up the bags:

"...exhibit 16-C, the stereo headphones with the cord which the defendant used to strangle Mr Kenneth Ockenden.

"...exhibit 16-D, the ligature the defendant utilized to murder Mr Stephen Sinclair.

"...exhibit 16-E, the set of rusty catering knives which the defendant used to dismember Mr John Howlett's body."

Raising this last plastic bag, the Detective Superintendent added, "The Crown would like to bring to the jury's attention that these knives previously belonged to one of the defendant's other victims, Mr Martyn Duffey. Mr Nilsen moved the knives from his apartment on Melrose Avenue to his flat at Cranley Gardens while having full mental awareness of his actions."

The Detective Superintendent Chambers also entered dozens of crime scene photographs into evidence, including the the stove upon which Nilsen had boiled the heads of his final three victims, the opening under the floorboards at Melrose Avenue, as well as the bath in which he had attempted to drown Carl Stottor and succeeded to drown John Howlett.

Jury members afterwards admitted that they became sick to their stomachs as the grisly story of twelve murders played out before them like a motion picture.

Once all the physical evidence and photographs had been introduced, Judge Croom-Johnson handed the court floor to the defense.

Dennis Nilsen's attorney stood up and said, "The defense calls Dr. James MacKeith, may it please Your Lordship."

"Continue, please," replied the judge.

MacKeith, a qualified psychiatrist, was sworn in and then gave his summary of the defendant's state of mind at the time of the killings:

"My Lord, I have examined Mr Nilsen and came up with the following fact: he had an extremely troubled childhood, something that caused him to have developed an inability to express cognitive emotional feelings. It is my professional opinion that this resulted in a separation of his mental function and his physical behavior, affecting his sense of identity and thereby implying diminished responsibility for his actions."

After MacKeith had given some more insights on his findings about Dennis Nilsen – not providing a formal diagnosis, though – the defense called a second psychiatrist, Dr. Patrick Gallwey, who had pretty much the same to say about Nilsen, but he also added a diagnosis:

"Mr Nilsen is suffering from a false self-syndrome, My Lord," he told the court. "This type of personality disorder often results in outbreaks of schizoid disturbances, which makes him incapable of premeditation. He acts on impulse and the vehemence of his actions can be attributed to his disturbed childhood as well as a lack of proper social interaction."

After hearing these somewhat technical testimonies from the two psychiatrists, the prosecution brought in their own rebuttal psychiatrist, Dr. Paul Bowden, who had also spent a fair amount of time (in excess of fourteen hours) examining Nilsen while he had been held at the Brixton correctional facility.

Speaking in a vernacular which the courtroom audience understood much better, Bowden dismissed both the claims that Dennis Nilsen suffered from a false self-syndrome and that he had an inability to express emotional feelings.

"Mr Nilsen has no form of disorder of the mind," he said in a firm tone of voice. "He forces himself to objectify other human beings."

Dr. Bowden further stated that, although Nilsen had certain abnormalities, he had a manipulative personality and he was capable of initiating relationships, therefor cognizant enough to take responsibility for his actions.

Bullshit, Dennis thought. *I have never manipulated anybody. I asked them to come to my home and they agreed. I have never forced anyone into doing anything they didn't want to.*

He looked sharply in the direction of the prosecuting attorney, who was leading the witness. *You can accuse me of murdering people, but don't accuse me of being manipulative, you jerk. I am Des Nilsen, a former civil servant of this city.*

CHAPTER 25

Members of the jury retired on November 3rd, 1983, to consider their verdict.

After deliberating for more than fourteen hours, they returned to the courtroom the next day, at 4:25 p.m. with a majority verdict of guilty on all six charges of murder and two charges of attempted murder: Carl Stottor and Douglas Stewart. It was another cold and miserable day in London and, by the time the court was in session again, it was almost completely dark outside.

"Has the jury reached a verdict?" Judge Croom-Johnson asked, adjusting his wig.

The jury foreman stood up and said, "We have, My Lord."

"What say you before the Old Bailey Central Criminal Court of England?"

Dennis Nilsen felt his knees buckle. *This is judgement day, Des,* he thought. *As from this moment you are going to answer for the unthinkable things you have done. Your life is over now.*

He could sense how the energy was draining from his scrawny body as the jury foreman said, "In the case of the Crown versus Nilsen, we, the jury, find the defendant, Dennis Andrew Nilsen, guilty of six counts of murder in the first degree and guilty of two counts of attempted murder."

Dennis stared at the jury foreman with cold eyes, thinking: *Six killings that the prosecution can prove, sure. What about the other six?*

On instruction from the judge, the jury foreman carefully approached the announcement bench and handed him the written verdict.

Judge Croom-Johnson didn't waste any time after that.

As soon as he had confirmed that the written verdict was in line with the spoken one, he peered over the rim of his eyeglasses and said in a serious tone: "Will the defendant please rise to receive the sentence decided upon by this court?"

Dennis gave an insecure nod and struggled to his feet. His shoulders were drooping and he appeared to be a shadow of the man he had once been.

The judge cleared his throat and then announced: "Dennis Andrew Nilsen, by the powers invested in me by the judicial system of England, I hereby sentence you to life in prison, with a twenty-five-year Tariff." When he noticed the frown on Nilsen's forehead, he asked, "Do you understand the sentence, Mr Nilsen?"

Shaking his head slowly, Dennis looked down at his quivering hands and said, "No, My Lord. What does the twenty-five-year Tariff mean?"

"It means, Mr Nilsen, that you will only be eligible to apply for parole after you have served a minimum of twenty-five-years of your sentence."

"I understand, My Lord," replied Dennis. Tears were welling up in his eyes.

The judge slammed down his gavel and said, "The court is now adjourned."

As people started filing out, Dennis asked his lawyer, bewildered, "Are they going to take me back to Brixton now?"

"No, you're going to Wormwood Scrubs in West London," his lawyer told him.

Dennis Nilsen's blood ran cold. From his days as a policeman, he recalled that Her Majesty's Prison Wormwood Scrubs was one of the roughest ones in England.

"Why there?" he inquired. "Why can't I stay at Brixton?" He desperately wanted to go back to Brixton Prison. After his stint in solitary confinement, he had made peace with some of the guards and they had been treating him well enough up to now. Wormwood Scrubs was going to be a different story, he had no doubt about it.

"You are a convicted murderer now, Des," said his lawyer. "Brixton is reserved for prisoners awaiting trial and yours is over. I'm sorry about your conviction, I did the best I could."

"It's all right," replied Dennis, "I deserve this. It's all my own fault."

He stood up and shook his lawyer's hand, before two police officers took hold of his arms and escorted him out of the courtroom.

This is it then, he thought as they walked through the doors, *finally the end of the road for me. Goodbye Bleep, I hope someone takes good care of you.* He would only find out later that Bleep was no longer alive by then.

Outside, the news reporters and journalists were in a frenzy. They were shouting and asking questions and waiving microphones around.

Dennis was overwhelmed by the attention. He gave a crooked smile and lifted his right hand in appreciation. One of the reporters looked like a nice enough fellow to Dennis and he cupped his ears to listen to the man's question.

"What is your response in regards to your life sentence?" the reporter asked.

"For me to be receiving any kind of sentence," Dennis replied, "I have to be *alive*." He sniffed. "That is twice as much as what my victims have. They are all dead and it's my fault."

Then he was bundled into the police car and on his way to the dangerous Wormwood Scrubs.

EPILOGUE

Dennis Nilsen was classified as a Category A prisoner at Wormwood Scrubs.

This meant that he could have his own cell, without having to share it with other prisoners, and that he had full access to all prison facilities where inmates were allowed.

Now that he knew he was going to be in a correctional facility for his entire life, his behavior toward the guards and other prison personnel improved dramatically. He wore his prison uniform, adhered to the rules and didn't cause any further problems – at least not for the next month and a half.

Upon arrival at the prison, he told his fellow inmates – who all knew him from watching the news – that the only reason he had failed to kill Carl Stottor and Paul Nobbs was that he had been too drunk. At thirty-seven years of age, Nilsen was older than a lot of the prisoners and he tried to befriend many of them; especially the ones in their early twenties.

On December 22nd, 1983, after an exercise period, Nilsen made advances of a homosexual nature toward twenty-one-year-old Albert Moffatt in the Wormwood Scrubs communal bathrooms. Young Albert, who was serving time for a robbery, declined politely but Dennis Nilsen lunged at him and he suddenly had to defend himself. He grabbed a razor blade, with his hand wrapped in a towel, and slashed Nilsen in the face and on his chest. The guards quickly came rushing in and stopped the fight after they had heard Nilsen's bloodcurdling screams.

He received eighty-nine stitches on his left cheek and his chest in the prison infirmary and was briefly transferred to the Parkhurst Prison on the Isle of Wight.

"I have no remorse about what I did," Albert Moffatt said after the incident. "The man is a monster. I would have no hesitation in doing it again. There should be an inquiry into why he was let loose inside among young men. He is clearly insane and should never be released."

Moffatt was not charged with assault after a jury decided that he had acted in self defense.

***

After his short stay at Parkhurst, Dennis Nilsen was transferred to Wakefield Prison, twenty-five miles north of Sheffield, where he remained for the following seven years. Here, again as a result of all the publicity surrounding his murders, Nilsen was threatened constantly by fellow inmates.

In 1991, after another attack by one of the inmates, he was moved to a vulnerable-prisoner unit at Full Sutton Prison, a maximum security facility near the city of York.

Toward the end of 1992, he was filmed in a short interview for the Carlton TV programme MURDER IN MIND. In this interview, Dennis Nilsen appeared calm and relaxed and talked about his crimes as if they were nothing more than everyday tasks.

"In the end, when there were two or three bodies under the floorboards," he told the reporter, "and it became summer, it got hot and then there would be a smell problem. I thought: what would cause the smell more than anything else? Then I came to the conclusion that it was the soft parts of the bodies; the organs. So, on a weekend, I would pull up the floorboards – blinding drunk because I found it totally unpleasant – and start dissection on the floor."

"What sort of preparation would you have to make for that?" the reporter asked incredulously.

Dennis interlocked his fingers on his lap. "Well, you know these plastic bags, the, uhm dustbin liners? You just split one of those so that it forms kind of a sheet. Then you put the body on the sheet and then… cut it up."

***

He stayed at Full Sutton Prison until 1993, when he was relocated to Whitemoor Prison, north of Cambridge, again as a Category A prisoner. At Whitemoor, the warden made sure Nilsen was mostly segregated from other inmates.

During his time at Whitemoor, he continued to monitor trade union activities and kept on challenging what he called "the abuse of prison rules" by guards and other correctional facility personnel. He sent dozens of letters to the European Court of Human Rights with protests regarding this matter. In one of these complaints, he said that his human rights had been violated when prison guards allegedly removed some of the more explicit pages from two softcore homosexual pornography magazines, *Him* and *Vulcan* – to which Dennis subscribed – before the magazines reached his cell.

Dennis Nilsen spent a lot of time writing while he was at Full Sutton Prison.

One of his major projects was an autobiography with the title *The History of a Drowning Boy*.

When he was asked about the name of his book, he explained that it had originated from two of his childhood experiences: one being his Grandfather, who had died while out at sea, the other one his own near-drowning experience, when the older boy with the strong hands and smooth body had saved his life.

In the autobiography it became clear that Nilsen's idea of life and death was intertwined between himself being alive and his Grandfather being dead. He also explained that, ever since he had left school, he lived two detached lives: his fantasy life and his real life.

When I was with people, I was in the "real" world, he wrote, *and in my private life, I snapped instantly into my "fantasy" life. I could oscillate between the two with instant ease.*

Writing about the murders he had committed, Nilsen blamed alcohol and his deranged emotional state for driving him to kill. He explained that the reason for his constant interaction with the dead bodies was that he was living out sexual fantasies, where he was the dominant older partner and the corpse the younger passive partner. These fantasies made him feel "adequate" for a change.

When Dennis Nilsen was finally ready to publish his autobiography early in 2001, the prison guards at Whitemoor confiscated the draft manuscript and turned it over to the police authorities. After a decision was made to prevent him from publishing the book, Dennis appealed to the European Court of Human Rights once again, saying that his rights to free speech had been violated by the decision.

***

Two years later, in 2003, he had still not heard back from the Human Rights Court. When he became frustrated and yelled at prison guards, he was reprimanded and transferred back to Full Sutton Prison again. He was fifty-seven years old at the time.

It was only three years after that – and a full twenty-eight years after the first murder – when Dennis Nilsen's initial victim, Stephen Holmes was formally identified. This identification was brought on by a combination of circumstantial evidence gathered and by a photograph of the fourteen-year-old youth which was shown to Dennis, whereupon he recognized the face and confirmed that is was indeed the boy he had strangled and drowned in a bucket of water in the winter of 1978.

During his second period at Full Sutton, Dennis had nothing significant to write anymore, since his story had already been put to paper, so he started working in the prison workshop where he translated books into braille for the blind inmates.

Some of his other hobbies included writing poetry, painting and composing music on a keyboard the warden allowed him to obtain.

***

On May 10th 2018, Dennis complained of severe stomach pains and was rushed to the York hospital where surgery was performed on him. There were complications, however, and a blood clot formed in one of his veins as a result.

Two days later, on May 12th 2018, Britain's most prolific serial killer to date, Dennis Andrew Nilsen, died at the age of seventy-two.

The History of a Drowning boy is still unpublished…

ABOUT THE AUTHOR

Robert Brown is an author and former freelance journalist in is mid-forties from California. Having been born and raised in the UK he moved to the US as a teenager with his family.

Robert moved back to the UK to pursue his dream to be a fulltime author. He lives in Liverpool with his wife and two children.

Robert has always been intrigued by true crime which led in part to his previous career of a freelance journalist writing for local publications primarily about unsolved murders. It was obvious to Robert that his passion for this genre would lead to him writing his first book "Deadly Illusions" in 2017.

Apart from writing Robert loves to spend time with his family and to indulge his other passion of the great outdoors. Having been raised in the UK it's no surprise that Robert is also a keen anglophile which is also reflected in his writing.

Robert has a unique writing style that uses both his UK and US backgrounds that creates stories that can be enjoyed by readers on both sides of the pond. Keep an eye out for further publications from Robert soon.

More Books by Robert Brown

Deadly Illusions: A Private Detective Crime Thriller

Purity Pursuit: A Gripping Crime Thriller (Private Detective Heinrich Muller Crime Thriller Book 1)

Beyond The Window: A Fast Paced Crime Thriller (Private Detective Heinrich Muller Crime Thriller Book 2)

Stolen Heritage: Gripping Crime Thriller (Private Detective Heinrich Muller Crime Thriller Book 3)

The People In The Woods: Fast Paced Crime Thriller

Blood Money: Page Turning Crime Thriller

Private Detective Heinrich Muller Collection

The Numbers Game: A Crime and Mystery Thriller

Made in the USA
Columbia, SC
25 September 2020